The Executor's Handbook

Second Edition

The Executor's Handbook

Second Edition

A STEP-BY-STEP GUIDE TO SETTLING AN ESTATE
FOR PERSONAL REPRESENTATIVES,
ADMINISTRATORS, AND BENEFICIARIES

THEODORE E. HUGHES
AND DAVID KLEIN

☑®

Facts On File, Inc.

This book is designed to provide accurate and authoritative information in regard to the subject matter covered. It is sold with the understanding that the author and the publisher are not engaged in rendering legal, accounting, or other professional service. If legal advice or other expert assistance is required, the services of a competent professional person should be sought.

THE EXECUTOR'S HANDBOOK: A Step-by-Step Guide to Settling an Estate for Personal Representatives, Administrators, and Beneficiaries

Facts On File, Inc.
132 West 31st Street
New York NY 10001

Library of Congress Cataloging-in-Publication Data

Hughes, Theodore E.
The executor's handbook: a step-by-step guide to settling an estate for personal representatives, administrators, and beneficiaries / Theodore E. Hughes and David Klein.
p.cm.
Includes index.
ISBN 0-8160-4426-0 (alk. paper)
1. Executors and administrators—United States—Popular works.
I. Klein, David, 1919–   II. Title.
KF778.Z9 H84 2001
346.7305'2—dc21   00-047708

Facts On File books are available at special discounts when purchased in bulk quantities for businesses, associations, institutions or sales promotions. Please call our Special Sales Department in New York at 212/967-8800 or 800/322-8755.

You can find Facts On File on the World Wide Web at
http://www.factsonfile.com

Text design by Erika K. Arroyo
Cover design by Cathy Rincon

Printed in the United States of America

MP FOF 10 9 8 7 6 5 4 3 2

This book is printed on acid-free paper.

CONTENTS

TABLES

FIGURES

A NOTE TO
THE READER

Although we have made every attempt to ensure that the information in this book is accurate, comprehensive, and current, we cannot predict the ways in which both state and federal laws may change, nor can we know the complexities of the estate with which you may be confronted.

For this reason, you must not consider this work as your accountant or lawyer in book form. Most estates are fairly simple and present no special problems. But if you find that the matters you are dealing with challenge your personal skills, you should not hesitate to retain professional help. The adage about an ounce of prevention has special relevance in connection with estate settlement, because it can bring to a swift conclusion probate proceedings that might otherwise drag on for months or years.

A word may be in order about the gender of our pronouns. In our efforts to maintain a minimally decent prose style, we have tried to avoid the awkward "he or she" as often as possible—especially when it is antecedent to the grammatically barbarous "they." Because males generally die at an earlier age than females, we have used "he" wherever we refer to the testator or the deceased. Similarly, we use "she" in reference to the surviving spouse. We hope that nobody takes offense at this seemingly sexist but basically sensible usage.

T. E. H.
D. K.

Part I

THE ROLE OF
THE EXECUTOR

~ 1 ~

WHEN DEATH OCCURS

An executor—or personal representative—is a person, bank, or trust company nominated in a will to carry out the wishes of the deceased and to do whatever is necessary to settle the deceased's probate estate. If a testator has nominated you to this position, what you can do, should do, and must do depends on when you are nominated; on your relationship with the testator—that is, the person who nominated you in his or her will—and on the nature and value of the testator's probate assets.

If, for example, you know months or years before the testator's death that you have been nominated, there is much that you can do to simplify—and perhaps eliminate—your job and to save the survivors a substantial amount of money in probate costs, death taxes, and other expenses, as well as the time and frustration of having to deal with a county court (usually called a probate court, but in some states called a surrogate, orphan's or chancery court). We will deal with this in detail in Chapter 3.

If you have a close relationship with the testator, you can play a supportive role at the time of death by helping to make funeral and burial arrangements, executing anatomic gifts, collecting nonprobate assets, and assisting the deceased's family and other survivors in various other ways, even though these activities are not legally required of executors. Chapter 4 will spell out what you can do in these respects.

But whether or not you do any of these things, your basic task is to carry out the terms of the will—that is, to locate and assemble the deceased's probate assets (see Chapter 5), to pay all taxes and legitimate debts, to protect the residue, and to distribute it to the beneficiaries designated in the will. Your work will be governed by the nature and value of the estate, by the terms of the will, and by state laws and court rules that govern the administration of decedents' estates. Hence, your first step in learning your role as executor is to understand the basic functions of a will and your role in settling the estate.

THE WILL

It is widely believed that only about one-third of all Americans die having drawn up and signed a will, and that the remaining two-thirds die intestate—that is, without a valid will. This statistic is correct only insofar as it refers to a formally executed will. But, in fact, everyone who dies has a will because, in the absence of a for-mally executed will, the state in which the deceased resided will impose one—that is, it will require any probate assets left by the deceased to be distributed in accordance with that state's intestacy laws. In either case, the appointment of an executor—or, to use the modern term, *personal representative*—will be necessary to carry out the probate court administration of any probate assets left by the deceased.

If we are to believe what we see in the movies or read in con-temporary novels, the reading of a will and the settling of an estate are rather simple processes. The cast of characters consists of a lawyer, who reads the will, and the deceased's survivors, some of whom are disgruntled at learning that they've been disinherited and others of whom leave the scene delighted with their generous bequests. In real life, however, the process is not that simple, because a will does much more than leave assets to specified ben-eficiaries, and the final settlement of an estate involves far more than the mere reading of a will.

BEQUEATHING THE ASSETS

The primary function of a will is to bequeath the testator's probate assets in virtually any way that he chooses. There are certain limi-tations. A will cannot, for example, be used to completely disinherit a spouse, or bequeath assets to an illegal organization, or impose on a bequest conditions that are regarded as socially undesirable ("I give my son $100,000 on condition that he divorce the woman to whom he is now married"). But the testator can disinherit one or more of his children, give more to one than to the others, leave money to a close but unrelated friend or to a shelter for homeless pets, or do virtually anything else with the probate assets that he leaves behind.

A state-imposed will is very different. Operating on the assumption that "blood is thicker than water," state intestacy laws may require that up to three-fourths of the probate assets go to the spouse, with the balance going to the deceased's descendants or parents. If the deceased leaves a spouse but no children or grandchildren, up to half may go to his parents. If there are no children or grandchildren, no surviving spouse, and no parents, the estate may go to brothers and sisters, nieces and nephews. And if there are no surviving relatives, the entire estate may go to the state. Under this statutory distribution formula, a surviving gay, lesbian, or other domestic partner gets nothing; neither does a close friend, an informally adopted child, an alma mater, or a favorite church or charity.

Whether or not there is a formally executed will, your responsibilities as executor include identifying and locating the beneficiaries and seeing that they receive the inheritance due them. Usually this is a simple process, but it can become tricky if one or more of them is difficult to locate, questions your authority to act, or contests the will or your proposal for paying claims or distributing the estate's assets.

PAYMENT OF DEBTS

A second function of the will is to direct that all lawful debts be paid by the estate—not merely such ordinary consumer debts as credit card balances, personal loans, and mortgage payments, but also final medical bills and funeral expenses. Here your task will involve notifying the deceased's creditors of the death, advising them of the time limits for submission of their claims, deciding which debts must be paid and which need not be, contesting debts which you believe are not legitimate, and paying those debts that have been determined to be legitimate. Chapter 8 deals with this procedure in detail.

DESIGNATION OF A GUARDIAN

If the testator has left minor or incompetent children orphaned by the death, the will has presumably nominated someone as their guardian to serve as a parent substitute until they reach the age of majority or attain competence. Here, again, in the absence of a will (or, in some states, a writing separate from a will) the probate court will propose a guardian, but this person may not be the one who would have been preferred by the deceased. The court almost invariably appoints a blood relative, whereas the deceased might have chosen a close friend with a more congenial lifestyle. As is sometimes the case, you, as executor, may also have been nominated as the guardian.

DESIGNATION OF A CONSERVATOR

Although the guardian usually takes charge of nominal assets (usually up to $5,000) inherited by minor children, the will may, if the value of the estate is substantial, nominate an individual or a bank or trust company to act as conservator—that is, to collect and manage a minor child's inheritance so as to preserve its value and maximize its yield until the child reaches the age of majority. There is no legal reason why the executor, the guardian, and the conservator cannot be the same person.

DESIGNATION OF AN EXECUTOR
(PERSONAL REPRESENTATIVE)

Every properly drafted will names some person or entity to carry out the terms of the will—to see that the will is probated; the probate assets collected, protected, and managed; the creditors notified of the death and invited to submit claims; the guardian and conservator formally appointed; the state and federal taxes paid; and, finally, the assets distributed to the beneficiaries as specified in the will or as prescribed by state law.

This person, known as the executor or personal representative, may be a friend or relative or, in the case of large estates, a bank or trust company. He or she may even be a beneficiary designated in the will. In any event, the executor functions basically as the "ghost" of the deceased, carrying out the terms of the will and settling the estate exactly as the deceased would if he could reappear after death.

Although, as we've noted, the executor may also serve as either guardian or conservator (or both) for minors, sometimes the person best qualified to be the executor is unsuited to the role of guardian or unwilling to take on its responsibilities; or the person named as guardian may be unwilling or unable to fulfill the role of executor.

If, as the executor, you must deal with a guardian or a conservator, bear in mind that your loyalty is to the deceased's estate and not to the guardian or conservator, and that you are duty bound not to alter the terms of the will, no matter how strongly you are urged to do so.

WHAT THE EXECUTOR DOES

If the will has designated you as the executor, and if the estate includes probate assets (see Chapter 5), you must file in probate court a petition for commencement of proceedings (see Chapter 2) in which you ask the court to confirm your nomination and appoint you as executor, admit the will to probate, and determine the persons entitled to inherit the probate estate. This involves demonstrating to the court's satisfaction that the will (including any amendments) was properly executed and is, indeed, the deceased's "last will and testament." If there is no will but there are probate assets, and you wish to serve as executor, the petition must include a request that you be appointed executor. Otherwise the court may appoint a total stranger—sometimes a political hack or a courthouse crony—possibly at excessive cost to the estate.

Once it has confirmed your nomination and appointed you as executor, the court will issue you "letters of authority"—a one-page document that certifies your authority to act on behalf of the estate in managing and disposing of the assets, opening and closing bank accounts, filing tax returns and paying taxes, and dealing with creditors, beneficiaries, and other interested persons. For example, by presenting your letters of authority, you can transfer into the estate's bank account cash on hand, certificates of deposit, salary checks, dividends, brokerage proceeds, and other probate funds owned by or owing to the deceased.

If all the estate's probate assets are liquid (such as bank and mutual fund account balances), your task is relatively simple. But when they include securities or real estate, you must decide whether to liquidate them immediately or hold them until a time when they might yield a higher price. Meanwhile you must monitor the securities and manage the real estate (paying mortgage payments, taxes, insurance premiums, utility bills, and other costs) until the property is sold or distributed to the beneficiaries.

If the deceased left as a probate asset a business or a professional practice in the form of a sole proprietorship, a partnership, or a corporation, your task will be more complicated, since you will have to decide whether the business should be carried on, liquidated immediately, or sold as a going concern.

Identifying, assembling, and managing the deceased's probate assets constitute only one part of your responsibilities. The deceased's liabilities also require attention. Not only must all of the deceased's current debts be paid from the estate's assets but also you must, by means of a published notice, inform creditors of the death and invite their submission of claims against the estate within the state-specified claims period (see Chapter 8). In addition, you must pay all taxes—real estate, state and federal income, and any state and federal death taxes—that the deceased owed at the time of death or for which the deceased, the estate, and the inheriting beneficiaries are liable.

While this financial process is taking place, you must locate and notify all persons whom the will names as beneficiaries, and any heirs at law (surviving spouse and next of kin), whether or not they are designated in the will. Normally, this is a simple task, but occasionally heirs at law are difficult to locate. Moreover, a disinherited survivor (for example, an estranged child) may decide to oppose your appointment, propose an alternative candidate, contest the will, or object to some or all of your actions in settling the estate.

Once the estate's probate assets have been collected and the liabilities discharged, you must distribute the residue to the entitled beneficiaries, file an accounting with the court, and obtain a court order closing the estate and discharging you from further responsibilities.

SHOULD YOU TAKE ON THE JOB?

This brief overview of the executor's role cannot do justice to the many details, which will be covered fully in subsequent chapters. On the one hand, for the sake of clarity, we have necessarily oversimplified aspects of the executor's task. On the other hand, in our attempt to delineate the executor's responsibilities in worst-case scenarios, we may have intimidated you unduly. As we shall note, the executor can call on a wide variety of professional advice and expertise and a satisfactory fulfillment of the role requires only an effective blend of conscientiousness, integrity, and common sense.

Although in some cases an executor first discovers his or her nomination after the testator has died, in most cases the testator asks the prospective executor or personal representative—usually when a will is contemplated, drafted, or revised—whether he or she is willing to serve. Of course, you can decline to serve in the first place or at some later stage, and you have every right to decline the nomination after the testator's death, or to resign after the probate court has formally appointed you.

There may be good reasons for you to decline to serve. If, for example, you are considerably older than the testator, or you are in poor enough health to worry about predeceasing him, or you foresee conflicts or other difficulties in dealing with creditors, beneficiaries, or other interested parties—or if you simply don't want the responsibility—it would probably be wise to decline the nomination.

But some of your reservations about serving may not be valid. As we have noted, if the estate is in any way complicated, you have the right to hire a wide array of experts to help you—probate lawyers, for example, or appraisers, accountants, real estate brokers, stockbrokers, or financial consultants—and to pay their fees from estate funds. If you have an orderly mind, reasonable prudence, and a willingness to deal with details, there is no reason for you to have reservations about serving. And if you are a close friend or a relative of the deceased, serving as his executor may prove to be a gratifying way of paying your last respects.

Of course, it is possible to simplify your task—or to eliminate it altogether—if the testator has taken you into his confidence early on. If, before the death, you can organize the testator's assets in ways that make probate administration extremely simple or that can eliminate it altogether, you will have earned the testator's gratitude before the death, provided an invaluable service to the survivors, and saved yourself considerable time and effort after the death. Chapter 3 describes some of the ways in which you can do this.

☞ 2 ☜
BECOMING AN EXECUTOR

Every properly drafted will nominates an executor—often referred to as a personal representative. On the death of the testator, this person will stand in the place of the deceased and do everything necessary to carry out the provisions of the will and settle the probate estate.

Ideally, this chapter should be read by the testator rather than by the person who has been nominated to serve, so that he fully understands the duties and responsibilities of the executor. But because you may be nominated to serve by someone who has not fully considered the responsibilities involved and the qualifications needed, you should review them yourself before accepting or declining the nomination. Armed with this information, if you accept the nomination you can do so with a fair amount of confidence that you can do the job. On the other hand, if you conclude after reading this chapter that you have substantive reasons for declining to serve, you are less likely to offend the testator who has asked you and more likely to be equipped to help him make a sounder choice.

THE EXECUTOR'S QUALIFICATIONS

A MATTER OF AGE

One of the more desirable qualifications of an executor is that he or she be junior to—and thus likely to outlive—the testator. Life expectancy is, of course, largely unpredictable, but an age gap of 10 years or more between the testator and the executor can be a reassuring safety factor. Minors, however, are not authorized to serve as executors.

Because most of us tend to choose as our closest friends people of our own age, and because some of us have misgivings about "the younger generation," it is often difficult for an older testator to name as executor someone considerably junior. The testator could, of course, nominate an adult child, a lawyer, a bank, or a trust company, but each of these choices has, as we shall see, disadvantages of its own.

If, then, you are asked to serve as executor by someone close to your own age, you should point out the problem and urge the testator to name an alternative should you predecease him. This is why a properly drafted will should always name a successor executor.

A MATTER OF RESIDENCE

It is important, too, that you be able to be close at hand at the time the testator dies—even though this is somewhat unpredictable. If, for example, you live in a distant state, or if your work entails a good deal of unavoidable travel, you should pause before accepting the invitation, because settling the estate may require you to be at the site of death continuously or intermittently for a considerable length of time. In addition, the cost of your travel to and from the deceased's state of domicile (where the estate must be probated) can deplete the estate's assets.

Some states disqualify nonresidents from serving as executors. Others permit nonresidents to serve but require that a "resident agent" be appointed in the domicile state over whom the local court will have personal jurisdiction.

A MATTER OF RELATIONSHIP

When drafting a will, many testators consider naming a spouse, sibling, or adult child as the executor—any of whom may, in addition, be a beneficiary named in the will. There is, in fact, no legal reason why a relative of the testator or a beneficiary of the estate cannot serve as executor. And since a close relative is likely to serve without having to post a bond and without charging a fee (see p. 15), the resulting savings to the estate can be considerable.

When family relationships are cordial and stable, the choice of a family member or a beneficiary as executor can be a sound one—

especially if the person chosen has some familiarity with the testator's assets; but in some cases it is an infallible recipe for strife and contention. Although an executor is duty bound to carry out the provisions of the will, some discretion is often necessary, and if siblings or other relatives are among the beneficiaries, various jealousies may surface and can, in some circumstances, generate lawsuits among the interested parties or against the executor and the estate.

If, then, you are asked to serve as executor for a parent, an uncle or aunt, or a sibling, you need to consider very carefully the family climate in which you will have to function. If you follow conscientiously the provisions of a carefully drafted will, you should, ideally, encounter no difficulty and expose yourself to no legal liability. But there is no way in which you can immunize yourself against the irrational behavior of beneficiaries (or nonbeneficiaries) who are your kith and kin.

A MATTER OF SKILLS

If the testator's assets are either substantial or complicated—involving residential and commercial real estate, for example, or a wide and varied portfolio of stocks, bonds, and limited partnerships, or an operating business—you may consider declining to serve on the grounds that you lack the necessary professional competence. In such a situation, you may suggest to the testator that he nominate a bank or a trust company as executor, but the fees charged for such services can be substantial, especially if the estate is not large, and the care with which the estate is supervised may be proportionate to its size.

It is important to recognize that as executor you will be entitled to hire whatever professional expertise is necessary to protect or maximize the value of the estate, to carry out your other responsibilities, and, if necessary, to file or defend against lawsuits. As the executor, you are authorized to employ or consult lawyers to handle all legal matters (including probate administration), appraisers for real estate and other estate assets, accountants to handle bill payments and tax matters, and financial advisers for the management or liquidation of securities, an ongoing business, or other assets. The cost of these services is payable with estate funds. In short, legal, financial, and business expertise is far less important than common sense, integrity, conscientiousness, and persistence.

YOUR RIGHT TO RENOUNCE

Bear in mind, too, that you have the right not only to decline the invitation at the outset but also to withdraw as executor at any time—even after you have been formally appointed by the court and have begun the settlement of the estate. Obviously, your withdrawal in midstream can disrupt the administration and settlement of the estate, but it is important to understand that you have an escape hatch, since you cannot foretell what may occur in your own life at an unknown time in the future.

YOUR DUTIES WHEN DEATH OCCURS

In general, as executor, you can expect to assume the following responsibilities on the testator's death:

- Identifying, collecting, and protecting the deceased's probate assets;
- If the probate estate includes real estate, securities, or an ongoing business, managing these assets until the estate is settled;
- Notifying the deceased's creditors of the testator's death and offering them an opportunity to present their claims;
- Filing federal and state income, estate, or inheritance tax returns;
- Paying the deceased's debts, taxes, and other expenses;
- Distributing the remaining assets to the beneficiaries according to the terms of the will or according to a settlement agreement executed by all beneficiaries.

This listing (and Table 2.1) outline the executor's responsibilities. Whether the task is simple or onerous, brief or lengthy, depends on the value and nature of the probate estate, the complexity of the deceased's business activities, and the reasonableness of the surviving interested persons. In a few cases the executor can expect to be involved for many months, and even years, but in the vast majority of cases the estate can be settled simply and quickly—and in some cases, as we shall see in Chapter 6, without the executor's having to take up the role at all.

THE EXECUTOR'S FEE

You are entitled to a fee for your services, and to reimbursement for all expenses—legal help, court costs, brokers' commissions, appraisals, and so on—that you incur in administering and settling the estate. In all states, this fee is set by law as "reasonable" compensation or as a percentage of the value of the estate's assets—but in all cases subject to court approval. Table 2.2 summarizes the state laws that specify the executor's fee.

If the will specifies an executor's fee in actual dollars, you can, in some cases, ignore this figure if it is less than a "reasonable" fee. On the other hand, if you are a beneficiary, you may decide to waive all or any part of the executor's fee, because this fee is subject to federal and state income taxes as ordinary income, whereas the inheritance taxes imposed by the state of domicile, if any, are generally lower.

LIABILITY OF THE EXECUTOR

Once you assume the role of executor, you will be carrying out your duties under the supervision of the probate court. You will be considered a fiduciary (one holding a position of great trust) and, as such, you will be expected to manage the assets, pay taxes and legitimate claims, and carry out the directives of the will, as far as possible, diligently, loyally, and prudently. And if you violate these standards—vague though they may seem—you open yourself to several punitive measures.

For one thing, if you manage the estate so as to waste assets or otherwise deprive the beneficiaries or the creditors of their rights, they may sue you. In addition, the court may order you to forfeit your compensation. And you can be removed by the court if it determines that such action would be in the best interests of the estate, the beneficiaries, or the creditors. The estate itself, however, can be protected against your negligence or malfeasance if you purchase a surety bond, which reimburses it for any losses. The cost of the bond is also payable from estate funds (see p. 22).

LOYALTY—AND CONFLICT OF INTEREST

It is essential that all persons interested in the estate have full confidence in the integrity of the executor, who serves in a fiduciary

TABLE 2.1
The Executor's Duties—A Summary

Studies Will and Letter of Instruction

- Meets with family, lawyer, and other interested persons to discuss estate, identify beneficiaries, and determine needs of survivors.
- Determines need to protect minor or incompetent survivors through appointment of guardian or conservator.
- Notes special instructions for anatomical gifts, body disposal, and funeral rites.
- Confers with and, if necessary, employs lawyer to represent executor.

Identifies, Collects, and Safeguards Assets

- Notifies post office to forward mail to the executor.
- Searches for assets. Reviews bank records and files. Opens safe deposit box.
- Inspects and secures real estate; continues or terminates utilities.
- Files claims for Social Security, veterans, retirement, and other benefits.
- Examines fire and casualty insurance policies and considers new or increased coverage.
- Evaluates going business and makes preliminary management decisions.
- Inspects and protects collectibles.
- Evaluates possible wrongful-death claim; preserves evidence, and commences suit if warranted.

Avoids or Minimizes Probate

- Identifies jointly held assets, which pass without probate to surviving joint owner.
- Identifies pay-on-death bank accounts and transfer-on-death securities, which pass without probate to designated beneficiaries.
- Identifies trust-held assets, which pass without probate to beneficiaries designated in the trust document.
- Identifies life insurance (not payable to the estate), which passes without probate to surviving beneficiaries designated in the policy.
- Identifies IRA, Keogh, SEP, deferred compensation, and other accounts (not payable to the estate), which pass without probate to surviving beneficiaries designated in the account.
- Appraises jointly owned and trust-held assets for tax purposes.
- Considers use of transfer by affidavit and other small-estate transfer procedures.

Initiates Formal Probate Administration

- Meets with lawyer to determine need for probate administration and legal representation.
- Petitions court for formal appointment as executor and issuance of letters of authority.
- Purchases executor's bond if required.
- Identifies interested persons and notifies them of proceedings.
- Petitions court to admit (approve) the will.
- Defends estate against will contests if any.
- Commences ancillary probate proceedings for out-of-state real property.

Assembles and Inventories Probate Assets

- Collects bank accounts, securities, income, life insurance (payable to the estate), debts owed to the deceased, and other probate assets.
- Appraises probate assets and files inventory with the court.
- Opens executor's bank account for deposit of estate funds.
- Estimates cash needed for debts, taxes, administration expenses, and distribution of bequests.

Administers the Probate Estate

- Analyzes securities and makes investment decisions.
- Evaluates ongoing business to determine whether to continue, sell, or liquidate it.
- Determines whether to keep or liquidate other probate assets.
- Seeks court approval of preliminary family allowance payments to surviving spouse or children.

Settles Creditors' Claims

- Publishes notice to creditors to submit their claims by specified date.
- If required, mails direct notice to all known creditors.
- Examines each submitted claim for validity and timeliness.
- Contests invalid or tardy claims.

Files Tax Returns and Pays Taxes

INCOME TAXES:
- Files deceased's final federal, state, and local income tax returns.
- Files estate's federal, state, and local income tax returns for income earned during probate administration.
- Appraises assets to establish stepped-up tax basis.
- Prepares for and handles audits by taxing authorities.

DEATH TAXES:
- Values estate assets for tax purposes.
- Files federal estate tax return if estate exceeds exclusion amount (see Chap. 9).
- Decides whether estate administration expenses should be deducted against federal income or estate tax.
- Files state inheritance or estate tax return if required.

Distributes Assets, Obtains Discharge, and Closes Estate

- Prepares final accounting, which reports all receipts and disbursements.
- Seeks court approval of executor's and lawyer's fees.
- After payment of debts, taxes, and expenses, distributes balance of probate estate to entitled beneficiaries and obtains receipts.
- If required by law, obtains court order discharging the executor and closing the estate.

relationship to the estate. Thus, the executor must be totally loyal to the estate and to the interests of the beneficiaries and the creditors, and must not personally profit from any transactions made on behalf of the estate.

In general, unless the will expressly permits it or the court approves it, the executor must not directly purchase or be interested in purchasing any estate assets, nor may he speculate with estate assets or invest them in his own trade or business. Even if an executor subsequently purchases an estate asset from another person, the purchase will be deemed void unless the title to the asset passed through a bona fide purchaser who paid fair market value and was unaware of the executor's interest. However, sale of the estate's assets to relatives of the executor has sometimes been approved when the purchase price was fair and it was established that all parties acted in good faith.

TABLE 2.2
Executors' Fees

State	Executor's Fee
Alabama	Just and fair amount up to 2.5% of receipts and disbursements.
Alaska	Reasonable compensation.
Arizona	Reasonable compensation.[1]
Arkansas	Up to 10% of first $1,000 of personal property; 5% of next $4,000; 3% of balance plus reasonable additional fee for services involving real estate.
California	Up to 4% of first $15,000; 3% of next $85,000; 2% of next $900,000; 1% of next $9,000,000; 0.5% of next $15,000,000; plus reasonable fee for the balance.
Colorado	Reasonable compensation.[1]
Connecticut	Reasonable compensation.
Delaware	Combined executor's and attorney's fees up to $250 plus 11.3% of amount over $2,000 for estates under $5,000; $565 plus 6.8% of amount over $5,000 for estates under $10,000; $905 plus 5.6% of amount over $10,000 for estates under $20,000; $1,465 plus 5.1% of amount over $20,000 for estates under $30,000; $1,975 plus 4.5% of

TABLE 2.2
Executors' Fees *(continued)*

State	Executor's Fee
	amount over $30,000 for estates under $40,000; $2,425 plus 3.9% of amount over $40,000 for estates under $60,000; $3,205 plus 3.7% of amount over $60,000 for estates under $80,000. For fees on larger estates, see court rules.[2]
District of Columbia	Reasonable compensation.
Florida	Reasonable compensation.[1]
Georgia	2.5% of money received and paid out plus additional fee for extraordinary services.
Hawaii	Reasonable compensation.[1]
Idaho	Reasonable compensation.[1]
Illinois	Reasonable compensation.
Indiana	Reasonable compensation.[1]
Iowa	Reasonable compensation not to exceed 6% of first $1,000; 4% of next $4,000; 2% over $5,000.
Kansas	Reasonable compensation.[1]
Kentucky	Up to 5% of value of personal property plus 5% of income collected.[2]
Louisiana	2% of value of estate, or higher reasonable fee if specified in will and approved by survivors.
Maine	Reasonable compensation.[1]
Maryland	Up to 9% of first 20,000; $1,800 plus 3.6% of amount over $20,000, unless higher fee specified in will.
Massachusetts	Such compensation as court may allow.
Michigan	Reasonable compensation.
Minnesota	Reasonable compensation.[1]
Mississippi	Court fixes fee at its discretion.
Missouri	Up to 5% of first $5,000; 4% of next $20,000; 3% of next $75,000; 2.75% of next $300,000; 2.5% of next $600,000; 2% of amount over $1,000,000.[1,2]
Montana	Up to 3% of first $40,000; 2% of amount over $40,000.[2]
Nebraska	Reasonable compensation.[1]

TABLE 2.2
Executors' Fees (continued)

State	Executor's Fee
Nevada	4% of first $15,000; 3% of next $85,000; 2% on excess over $100,000, or higher fee if specified in will.
New Hampshire	Reasonable compensation.
New Jersey	5% of first $200,000; 3.5% of excess up to $1,000,000; 2% on balance.[2]
New Mexico	Reasonable compensation.[1]
New York	5% of first $100,000 received and paid out; 4% of next $200,000; 3% of next $700,000; 2.5% of next $4,000,000; 2% of amounts over $5,000,000.
North Carolina	Up to 5% of receipts and expenditures. On estates of less than $2,000, clerk sets fee.
North Dakota	Reasonable compensation.[1]
Ohio	4% of first $100,000; 3% of next $300,000; 2% of balance, determined with reference to personal property, income received, and proceeds of real estate.[2]
Oklahoma	5% of first $1,000; 4% of next $5,000; 2.5% of excess over $6,000.[1,2]
Oregon	7% of first $1,000; 4% of next $9,000; 3% of next $40,000; 2% on amount over $50,000; plus 1% of property subject to inheritance or estate tax.[1,2]
Pennsylvania	Reasonable compensation.
Rhode Island	Reasonable compensation.
South Carolina	Up to 5% of personal property plus 5% of proceeds of sold real estate plus 5% of income earned by the estate.[2]
South Dakota	Reasonable compensation.[1]
Tennessee	Reasonable compensation.
Texas	5% of incoming and outgoing cash.
Utah	Reasonable compensation.[1]
Vermont	$4 per day while performing duties of office.[2]
Virginia	Reasonable compensation.
Washington	Reasonable compensation.
West Virginia	Reasonable compensation (usually 5% of receipts).
Wisconsin	2% of estate, less mortgage and liens plus higher fee if approved by majority of beneficiaries.

TABLE 2.2	
Executors' Fees *(continued)*	
State	Executor's Fee
Wyoming	10% of first $1,000; 5% of next $4,000; 3% of next $15,000; 2% of amount over $20,000.[2]

[1] Executor may renounce fee limits in will and collect higher fee allowed by state law unless compensation is set by contract.

[2] Court may award higher fee.

PRUDENCE

In carrying out his duties, the executor is only required to exercise the care, judgment, and skill which the "ordinary prudent man" brings to bear in transacting his own business. As long as such care is exercised, the executor cannot be faulted for failure either to make profits on the estate's assets or to avoid reasonable losses. However, he can be held liable for continuing to allow the estate's assets to be diminished by an unwise investment after having become aware of the financial risks involved.

In order to protect against possible liability, the executor should, prior to settling the estate, invest all liquid assets in federally insured instruments, even though more speculative instruments promise a substantially higher yield. Similarly, if the will specifies that the estate's securities are to be sold immediately after death, the executor should sell them promptly rather than trying to outguess the market.

PROTECTION FOR THE EXECUTOR

There are several ways in which the executor can be protected against claims of malfeasance or negligence. Some of these must be put in place before the testator's death; others can be established afterwards.

PROVISIONS IN THE WILL

The testator can, in the will, include provisions which, in their absence, might expose the executor to personal liability. For example, the will could authorize the executor to make investments which, without such express permission, state law governing executors might prohibit as being too speculative. Similarly, the will may expressly authorize self-dealing by the executor, although this will always be subject to close scrutiny by the court.

CONSENT OF THE BENEFICIARIES

The executor planning to liquidate the deceased's securities portfolio or art collection, or to make an early partial distribution to beneficiaries, can avoid subsequent questions and conflict about these actions by first obtaining written approval of his actions from all interested parties.

COURT ORDERS

If, after all interested parties have been notified, the executor obtains a court order for a specific course of action, he will be protected against future liability.

SETTLEMENT AGREEMENTS

Occasionally in the course of settling an estate, disagreements arise between the executor and the beneficiaries or the creditors. In such circumstances, a written out-of-court settlement agreement among the interested parties is a binding instrument that protects the executor against future liability.

BONDING

Perhaps the strongest safeguard an executor can have against beneficiaries' or creditors' allegations of negligence or malfeasance is a surety bond—a form of insurance that will compensate the estate for any losses due to fraud, embezzlement, or negligence on his part. Although the will may specify that the executor may serve without bond, the probate court may nevertheless order that a bond be posted if it believes it necessary for the protection of the beneficiaries and the creditors. In any event, the cost of bonding the executor is payable with estate funds. On the other hand, if the will does not waive bonding, the court may do so—especially if the executor is also the sole beneficiary of the estate.

Bonding is easy to arrange through most insurance agents. But, despite the pressure of time, some shopping around is advisable— as it is in the purchase of any other kind of insurance. The bond premium is based on the value of the estate's assets, but if the value of the assets is substantial, a discount on the premium can sometimes be negotiated with an agent who is especially eager to sell the coverage.

The bond premium is payable annually until the estate is settled and closed. Because it may be renewed automatically, the executor should cancel the bond as soon as the estate is closed by sending the insurance company a copy of the final "Court Order Discharging the Executor" (see Fig. 10.3) and requesting a refund of any unearned premium.

GETTING FORMALLY APPOINTED

In our attempt to provide an accurate picture of the executor's responsibilities, we may have inadvertently described a "worst-case scenario." Although a small minority of probate estates confront their executors with many of the problems we have outlined, the vast majority are settled smoothly and relatively easily. In fact, your next step, once the testator has died, depends entirely on the nature and value of the estate's probate assets—a subject that is dealt with in detail in Chapter 6. At this juncture, we will outline the several alternatives that you may face.

First, you may discover that the deceased left no probate assets whatever, because all the assets consist of life insurance proceeds not payable to the estate, jointly held or trust-held assets, monies in accounts payable to designated beneficiaries, or securities in accounts transferable to designated beneficiaries (see p. 38). In this event, there is no need for you to serve at all, because the assets will be distributed to the life insurance beneficiaries, the surviving joint owners, or the trust designated or account-designated beneficiaries.

Second, the deceased may have left so few probate assets that they can be quickly distributed to the survivors by one of the "small estate" transfer procedures described in Chapter 6. In such cases, you may want to advise the beneficiaries about the procedure, but you will have no formal function to perform, because the settlement of some of the deceased's assets may be accomplished through use of a simple transfer affidavit. For other small estates, you may have to apply to the probate court for letters of authority (see p. 111) that authorize you to collect the deceased's individually owned assets. Once these are in your hands, you can distribute them to the beneficiaries and quickly close the estate. Lastly, you may find that the deceased left substantial probate assets, in which case you will need to assume the formal role of executor.

Although the deceased's will *nominated* you as the executor, you cannot assume your role until your nomination has been approved by order of the probate court. This procedure, along with a detailed description of your duties and responsibilities, is presented step by step in Chapter 7. Before reading it, however, you can discover, in the next chapter, how these duties can be significantly reduced or eliminated if you have the opportunity to discuss the estate with the testator before death occurs.

3

STRATEGIES BEFORE DEATH

Life being unpredictable, death may occur at any time. But if you have been nominated as executor when the testator is still in good health, can anticipate a normal life expectancy, and is receptive to your advice, there is much that you can suggest that will make your ultimate task easier and will benefit the testator's survivors.

THE LETTER OF INSTRUCTION

Although the testator has obviously made a will—otherwise you would not have been nominated as the executor—the will should make bequests in general terms and should not list every one of the testator's assets. Of course, the will can bequeath certain possessions (a piece of jewelry, for example, or an antique desk) to a specific individual, but if it were to list every asset it would have to be revised each time an asset is bought or sold, or each time the testator has a change of mind. But the testator's assets and liabilities should be enumerated in detail in another very useful document that relatively few testators prepare. This is the letter of instruction, which lists all the testator's assets and liabilities, specifies their location, and identifies their form of ownership—that is, whether they are owned solely, jointly, or in a trust, or are payable to a designated beneficiary (for example, life insurance and Keogh, IRA, SEP, and 401K accounts).

One of the more serious problems facing an executor after the testator's death is uncertainty or ignorance about the existence,

location, ownership, or current value of some assets—ranging from car keys to insurance policies. This may not be a problem if all assets were owned jointly and if the surviving joint owner was aware of all financial transactions; but if joint owners die simultaneously, or if the surviving joint owner paid little attention to "business matters," there is a real possibility that the executor will overlook some of the deceased's assets.

The letter of instruction will be helpful not only to you as the executor but also to the testator, because its periodic review can help determine not only his current net worth but also whether the current allocation of his assets is providing the best possible yield.

Unlike a will, the letter of instruction is not a legally enforceable document. It may take any of a number of forms. It can, for example, consist of an informal letter to survivors, a file of index cards, a loose-leaf notebook, or a computer disk, all of which are relatively easy to update (see Figure 3.1) *The Beneficiary Book* (P.O. Box 500028, San Diego, CA 92150—1-800-222-9125) offers a comprehensive fill-in-the-blanks letter of instruction in loose-leaf form. Personal Record (Nolo Press, 950 Parker St., Berkeley, CA 94710—1-800-992-6656), is a software program compatible with almost any computer. No matter what form it takes, the letter of instruction should be made accessible to you, as executor, immediately after the testator's death.

In addition to listing assets and liabilities, the letter of instruction can serve three other purposes. First, it can specify the testator's preferences as to funeral rites, burial, and anatomical gifts. The letter of instruction is a more appropriate place for this information than the will, because the will may not be discovered until after the funeral. The letter of instruction may well be more accessible and more likely to be read immediately after the death—especially if you, as the executor, know of its existence and location.

Figure 3.1
TOPICS FOR A LETTER OF INSTRUCTION

EMERGENCY INFORMATION	Address Book
People to Notify	Living Will
Child Care	Financial Power of Attorney
Child's Guardian	Health Care Power of Attorney
Animal Care	Other Emergency Information
Care of Property	

Figure 3.1
TOPICS FOR A LETTER OF INSTRUCTION *(continued)*

AVAILABLE MONEY
Checking Account
Savings Account
Money Market
Certificate of Deposit
Cash
Traveler's Checks
Automatic Teller
Debit Card
Other Available Money

SOURCES OF CURRENT INCOME
Employment
Pension
Independent Contractor
Trust Fund
Alimony
Child Support
Worker's Compensation
Insurance Settlement
Rental Income
Royalties
Dividends
Interest
Annuity
Other Sources of Income

PENSIONS/RETIREMENT ACCOUNTS
Social Security
Public Employment
Private Employment
Military
Union
IRA
Keogh
401(K) Plan
Other Pension/Retirement Account

SECURITIES
Stocks
Bonds
Mutual Fund
U.S. Notes/Bills/Bonds
Commodities

Other Securities

REAL ESTATE
Family Home
Vacation Home
Co-op/Condominium
Duplex
Rental Property
Tenant Information
Mobile Home/Lessor's Land
Mobile Home/Your Land
Timeshare
Undeveloped Land
Agricultural Land
Boat/Marina Dock Space
Airplane Hangar

BUSINESS INTERESTS
Sole Proprietorship
Partnership
Limited Partnership
Limited Liability Company
Corporation
Joint Venture
Collaboration Agreement
E-commerce Website
Other Business Interest

COPYRIGHTS, PATENTS, ETC.
Copyright
Patent
Trademark

VEHICLES/BOATS/PLANES
Motor Vehicle
Motorcycle
Motor Home/RV
Boat
Plane
Other Vehicles/Boats/Planes

HOME INVENTORY/VALUABLES
Antiques
Appliances
Art
Bedding

Figure 3.1
TOPICS FOR A LETTER OF INSTRUCTION *(continued)*

HOME INVENTORY/VALUABLES
Books
China/Pottery
Clothing
Coins
Collectibles
Computers
Crystal/Glassware
Electronic Equipment/TV/VCR
Floor Coverings
Furs
Furniture
Garden/Yard Items
Gems
Guns
Holiday Items
Jewelry
Living Things/Plants
Musical Instruments
Office Equipment
Pets
Photographic Equipment
Precious Metals
Recreation/Camping
  Equipment
Religious Items
Silver
Sports Equipment
Stamps
Tapes/CDs/Records
Tools/Work Equipment
Window Coverings
Wine/Liquor
Other Items/Miscellaneous

INSURANCE
Life
Homeowner/Renter
Medical
Vehicle
Disability
Annuity
Other Insurance

ADVISORS MONEY/TAX/LEGAL
Accountant
Real Estate Broker
Insurance Broker
Stockbroker
Auto Broker
Financial Advisor
Tax Preparer
Attorney
Other Advisors

PEOPLE/SERVICES/CONTRACTS
Child Care—In Home
Child Care—Away
Animal Care—In Home
Animal Care—Away
Cleaning Person
Gardener
Contractor
Repair Person
Pool Maintenance
Pest Control
Appliance Repair
Vehicle Repair
Other Services

TAX RECORDS
Current/Not Filed
Past Year/Not Filed
Filed

CREDIT CARDS
Bank
Department Store
Gasoline
Other Credit Card

WHAT YOU OWE
Monthly Bills
Rent
Money—Written Agreement
Money—Oral Agreement
Object—Written Agreement
Object—Oral Agreement
Court Judgment

Figure 3.1
TOPICS FOR A LETTER OF INSTRUCTION *(continued)*

WHAT YOU OWE
Retainer
Other You Owe

WHAT'S OWED YOU
Money—Written Agreement
Money—Oral Agreement
Object—Written Agreement
Object—Oral Agreement
Borrowed Object
Court Judgment
Retainer
Frequent Flyer Info
Other Owed to You

BURGLAR ALARMS
House
Vehicle
Business
Boat
Other Burglar Alarm

LOCKED PLACES/KEYS
Safe-Deposit Box
Post Office Box
Things Needing Keys
Combination Lock
Safe
Access Card/Code
Mini/Public Storage

HIDING PLACES
Hiding Place
Computer Password

MEDICAL INFORMATION
Family Practitioner
Specialist
Dentist
Eye Care Provider
Other Provider
Medical History
Immunization
Other

MEMORABILIA/THINGS
Photos

Letters
Movies/Videos
Cassettes
Mementos
Other Memorabilia/Things

PERSONAL DOCUMENTS
Birth Certificate
Passport
License
Marriage/Divorce
Nuptial Agreement
Cohabitation Agreement
Immigration/Naturalization
Other Legal
Educational
Professional
Employment
Religious
Ceremonial
Military
Other Personal Documents

PERSONAL INFORMATION
Personal Data
Employment History
Education
Military Record
Past Residence
Marriage
Former Marriage
Significant Relationship
Former Significant Relationship
Other Personal Information

YOUR FAMILY
Immediate Family—Living
Immediate Family—Deceased
Ancestor
Other Your Family

DEATH PLANS
Organ Donation
People to Notify
Body Disposition

Figure 3.1	
TOPICS FOR A LETTER OF INSTRUCTION *(continued)*	
DEATH PLANS	ESTATE MATTERS/WILL
Obituary/Death Notice	Will
Funeral/Service Details	Codicil
Obituary/Death Notice	Trust Documents
Funeral/Service Details	Trustee
Pre-need Contract	Executor/Personal Representative
Burial Insurance	Guardian/Conservator
Final Resting Place	Estate Planning Attorney
Epitaph	Letter of Instruction
Memorial Service	List of Assets
Other Death Plans	Other Estate Matters/Will

Unlike the will, the letter of instruction can take any form. This menu, adapted from the software program Personal Record, can serve as a useful guide to the scope and depth of the letter. *Reprinted by permission of Nob Press.*

The letter of instruction is also the appropriate medium for any "message to the world" that the testator would like to leave. This should not be incorporated into the will because, should the estate require probate, the will becomes a public document, accessible by anyone.

Lastly, the letter of instruction can be of great help to the executor and other survivors by providing a wide variety of information that they may not be aware of: when the car is due for its next oil change; where the home circuit breaker and water shutoff valve are located; whom to call to service the lawn mower; how to turn on the personal computer and access secure data; how and when to service the swimming pool and the smoke alarms; where the negatives of photographs are filed. This information may seem trivial, and in some cases unnecessary, but the lack of it often adds to the stress experienced by the survivors.

The menu shown in Figure 3.1 is not intended as a prescription. Rather it is offered as a checklist to suggest the kinds of entry that should be made in most such documents.

DURABLE POWER OF ATTORNEY

Another very useful document that should be prepared before death is the durable power of attorney. This document, when signed by the grantor, gives one or more agents the authority to act on the grantor's behalf in specified circumstances. (Despite the name of the document, these agents need not be attorneys.) Many spouses routinely give each other their power of attorney.

A power of attorney may be limited to a specified period of time (for example, during the grantor's hospitalization) or to a specific purpose (for example, the sale of the grantor's house or the management of his brokerage account) or to specified circumstances (for example, if the grantor becomes incompetent).

Historically, a power of attorney was automatically revoked if the grantor became incompetent. Today, however, many states recognize a "durable" power of attorney (see Figure 3.2), which survives incompetence if the grantor expressly states this preference in the document. Your local probate court clerk can tell you whether your state recognizes the durable version.

The durable power of attorney is especially important for all adults, because, in addition to designating another to make financial decisions, it can authorize the designated agent to make decisions about continuing or withholding medical treatment should the grantor become incompetent.

Although a living will (see below) may also state one's preference regarding health care, a medical power of attorney has been recognized by physicians and hospital authorities.

THE LIVING WILL

If, at the end of their lives, they should become comatose or terminally ill, some people would prefer to have all medical treatment withdrawn so that they can die quickly. Others would prefer that every possible heroic measure be taken to prolong their lives. Unless clear and unambiguous information has been recorded about such preferences, the survivors and the attending physician are often left quite uncertain about which course to follow. Some survivors would prefer to terminate the life but are agonizingly unsure about the patient's preferences. And some physicians are concerned about being sued for malpractice or, worse yet, criminally prosecuted for homicide.

Figure 3.2

DURABLE POWER OF ATTONEY

I, JOHN WILLIAMS, residing at 12 Pine, Okemos, Mich., hereby appoint MARY WILLIAMS, of the same address, my true and lawful attorney-in-fact for me and in my name, place, and stead, and for my use and benefit:

To exercise, do, or perform any act, right, power, duty, or obligation whatsoever that I now have or may acquire the legal right, power, or capacity to exercise, do, or perform in connection with, arising out of, or relating to any person (including myself), item, thing, transaction, business, property, real or personal, tangible or intangible, or matter whatsoever;

To ask, demand, sue for, recover, collect, receive, and hold and possess all such sums of money, debts, dues, bonds, notes, checks, drafts, accounts, deposits, legacies, bequests, devises, interests, dividends, stock certificates, certificates of deposit, annuities, pension and retirement benefits, insurance benefits and proceeds, documents of title, chooses in action, personal and real property, intangible and tangible property and property rights, and demands whatsoever, liquidated or unliquidated, as are now or shall hereafter become due, owing, payable, owned, or belonging to me or in which I have or may acquire an interest, and to have, use, and take all lawful ways and means and legal and equitable remedies, procedures, and writs in my name for the collection and recovery thereof, and to compromise, settle, and agree for the same, and to make, execute, and deliver for me and in my name all endorsements, acquittances, releases, receipts, or other sufficient discharges for the same;

To lease, purchase, exchange, and acquire, and to bargain, contract, and agree for the lease, purchase, exchange, and acquisition of, and to take, receive, and possess any real or personal property whatsoever, intangible or tangible, or interest therein, on such terms and conditions, and under such covenants as said attorney in fact shall deem proper;

To improve, repair, maintain, manage, insure, rent, lease, sell, release, convey, subject to liens, mortgage, and hypothecate, and in any way or manner deal with all or any part of any real or personal property, intangible or tangible, for me and in my name, and under such terms and conditions, and under such covenants as said attorney shall deem proper;

To sign, endorse, execute, acknowledge, deliver, receive, and possess such applications, contracts, agreements, options, covenants, deeds, conveyances, trust deeds, security agreements, bills of sale, leases, mortgages, assignments, insurance policies, bills of lading, warehouse receipts, documents of title, bills, bonds, debentures, checks, drafts, bills of exchange, notes, stock certificates, proxies, warrants, commercial paper, receipts, withdrawal receipts and deposit instruments relating to accounts or deposits in, or cer-

Figure 3.2

DURABLE POWER OF ATTONEY *(continued)*

tificates of deposit of, banks, savings and loan or other institutions or associations, proofs of loss, evidences of debts, releases, and satisfaction of mortgages, judgments, liens, security agreements, and other debts and obligations, and such other instruments in writing of whatever kind and nature as may be necessary or proper in the exercise of the rights and powers herein granted;

To do or authorize any act over my person that I could do or authorize, including consenting to placing me in a home or hospital for care and otherwise providing for my care and authorizing medical and surgical treatment for me;

I grant to my said attorney-in-fact full power and authority to do and perform all and every act and thing whatsoever requisite, necessary, and proper to be done in the exercise of any of the rights and powers herein granted, as fully to all intents and purposes as I might or could do if personally present, with full power of substitution or revocation, hereby ratifying and confirming all that my said attorney in fact, or his substitute or substitutes, shall lawfully do or cause to be done by virtue of this power of attorney and the rights and powers herein granted.

This instrument is to be construed and interpreted as a general power of attorney over my person and property. The enumeration of specific items, acts, rights, or powers herein does not limit or restrict, and is not to be construed or interpreted as limiting or restricting the general powers herein granted to said attorney-in-fact.

This durable power of attorney shall not be affected by my disability except as provided by statute.

The rights, powers, and authority of said attorney in fact to exercise any and all of the rights and powers herein granted shall commence and be in full force and effect on execution of this document.

Witnesses:

_____   _____

Jennifer M. Jones   John Williams

_____

Sarah D. Smith

STATE OF MICHIGAN   }
                    ss
COUNTY OF INGHAM }

Figure 3.2

DURABLE POWER OF ATTONEY *(continued)*

On this 1st day March, 1994, before me, a Notary Public in and for said County, personally appeared JOHN WILLIAMS to me known to be the same person described in, and who executed the within instrument, who acknowledged the same to be his free act and deed.

Ann McGill, Notary Public
Ingham County, Michigan
My Commission Expires: 2/15/02

Instrument Prepared By:
Laurence L. Lawyer
Attorney at Law
101 Capitol Avenue
Lansing, Michigan 48609

This dilemma is easily resolved, both for survivors and for the physician, by the execution of a living will, which states precisely the conditions under which treatment is to be withheld or terminated. In more than 40 states, some form of living will is legally binding on both the family and the attending physician, and in these states its execution cannot be interpreted as suicide by insurance companies that have a suicide clause in their life insurance policies. It seems clear that living wills will soon be recognized in all states.

Legal specifications for an enforceable living will vary from one state to another, but a form tailored to the specifications of your state can be obtained from an organization called Choice in Dying, 1035 30th St. NW Washington, D.C. 20007. The sample form shown in Figure 3.3 may satisfy the laws of your state. Many state laws require that the form be dated and signed in the presence of two witnesses who are not (1) related to the signer, (2) beneficiaries of the signer, or (3) the signer's attending physician or his employees. The form may need to be notarized and, if so, the notary may serve as one of the witnesses.

Because some states do not recognize a living will until the signer has been diagnosed as terminal, the living will should be updated periodically. Copies should be given to the signer's attend-

Figure 3.3

LIVING WILL

Being of sound mind, I willfully and voluntarily hereby make known my desire that my dying shall not be artificially prolonged under the circumstances set forth below:

If at any time I should have an incurable injury, disease, or illness, regarded as a terminal condition by my physician, and if my physician has determined that the application of life-sustaining procedures would serve only to artificially prolong the dying process and that my death will occur whether or not life-sustaining procedures are utilized, I direct that such procedures be withheld or withdrawn and that I be permitted to die with only the administration of medication or the performance of any medical procedure deemed necessary to provide me with comfort care.

In the absence of my ability to give directions regarding the use of such life-sustaining procedures, it is my intention that this declaration should be honored by my family and physician as the final expression of my legal right to refuse medical or surgical treatment and accept the consequences of such refusal.

I understand the full import of this declaration, and I am emotionally and mentally competent to make this declaration.

Signed _____   _____

The declarant has been personally known to me, and I believe him or her to be of sound mind.

_____   _____
                Witness   *Witness*

State of _____   _____

County of _____

Subscribed and sworn to before me on the _____ day of _____,

_____ .

_____

Notary Public, State of _____

My commission expires _____

ing physician for filing with the signer's medical record, to one or more members of the family, and perhaps to a trusted (and younger) friend. A copy should also be kept with the signer's will, the letter of instruction, and other important papers.

INSURANCE POLICIES

Life insurance policies may not provide significant protection beyond middle age because by that time children tend to be self-sufficient, mortgages are likely to have been paid off, and other assets have probably been acquired. As a consequence, many people in their fifties and sixties tend to cash in their policies or let them lapse.

Although they are not probatable (except when the estate or its executor is the named beneficiary), however, life insurance proceeds *are* considered part of a deceased's estate for federal estate-tax purposes. Inclusion of insurance proceeds in one's taxable estate can be avoided, however, if ownership of the policy is transferred to another person—presumably a beneficiary—while the insured is still alive. After the transfer, the insured may continue to pay the premiums, but the new owner must possess what the IRS terms all "incidents of ownership," including the right to change beneficiaries or even to cancel the policy. Ownership of the policy can be transferred by means of an assignment form, available from the insurance agent or the company.

CONVERTING THE ASSETS

Bear in mind that after the testator's death your major responsibilities will involve collecting, managing, and disposing of the *probate* assets. Hence, to the extent that you can persuade the testator to convert his assets from a probate to a *nonprobate* form, you will undoubtedly simplify—and perhaps even eliminate altogether—many of the problems and costs of probate administration, as well as your responsibility for settling the estate.

You may feel hesitant about suggesting the strategies outlined in this chapter because they inevitably require the testator to face the prospect of death. But if you bear in mind that the testator faced this prospect when he nominated you as executor, your concerns should diminish. You may also feel that advising the testator about converting his assets into nonprobate form involves an intrusion into his financial status and net worth. But this need not occur. You can, for example, explain the benefits of joint ownership or the advantages of a living trust—and even assist in the transfer of assets into these nonprobate forms—without having to learn the actual value of the assets.

Because every estate consists of a unique mix of assets, and because the ages of the survivors and their relationship to the testator will differ in each case and will change over time, the tactics suggested here will not be practical for every situation. It is almost certain, however, that some of these will make your ultimate task as executor significantly easier.

JOINT OWNERSHIP

Because only those assets held in the deceased's name alone are probatable, the need for eventual probate can be reduced or eliminated by converting solely owned assets into jointly owned assets. Under this form of ownership, sometimes called joint tenancy, the jointly owned assets pass directly to the surviving joint owner(s) on the death of any one of them—without the need for probate court administration.

Joint ownership can be established between or among any individuals—not only spouses and children but also unrelated friends. Hence it may be particularly useful for unmarried cohabitants, because if one member of the couple dies intestate and without having made other arrangements, the survivor would inherit none of the deceased's solely owned assets.

Joint ownership is easy enough to establish. On a bank account it simply involves changing the registration of the account to reflect joint ownership and adding the joint owner's name to the signature card. On securities, the transfer requires nothing more than a new and cost-free registration of the stock certificates or bonds or the brokerage account, and on real estate the execution and recording of a new deed indicating the joint ownership.

When an owner places money in a joint account, no gift tax accrues until the joint owner liquidates the account, but if the assets consist of real estate or securities, the tax accrues immediately.

Because it usually avoids probate, joint ownership has been called "the poor man's will," but, although it can be very useful, this form of ownership has some inherent limitations and disadvantages. These the owner must understand before adopting it is a probate-avoidance tactic.

To begin with, joint ownership may be irrevocable in the absence of the consent of all the joint owners. It thus involves some loss of control over the assets. For instance, if the owner establishes joint ownership of a house or condominium with a friend and subsequently they have a falling out, the friend retains an irrevocable interest in the jointly owned property unless and until he voluntarily consents to release it by signing and delivering a new deed.

In addition, if securities are placed in joint ownership with a minor child, they may be unsellable until the child reaches majority, because a minor is legally incapable of executing such a transaction. And any liquidation or conversion of jointly held assets may require the consent of all the owners.

Perhaps more important, because the sequence of deaths is unpredictable, complications may arise. For example, if a parent places a house in joint ownership with two adult daughters, intending that they and their children share equally in the property, and if one of the daughters predeceases the parent, the entire property will, on the parent's death, pass to the surviving daughter, who has no legal obligation to share the house or its proceeds with her deceased sister's children. Similarly, if the owner places assets in joint ownership with a spouse who then predeceases him, the assets revert to sole ownership by the survivor and hence become subject to probate on his death.

If both joint owners die simultaneously, jointly owned assets become probatable. And if the spouse survives, but not long enough to make a new will or provide otherwise, the assets will pass, if the couple was childless, to the surviving spouse's nearest relatives and not to the testator's. A more detailed discussion of simultaneous death appears on p. 200.

The tax consequences of joint ownership are somewhat complex. In general, setting up joint ownership with anyone who did not contribute to the purchase of the asset constitutes a gift equal to half its value. Hence, if the value of the asset exceeds $10,000, it is subject to the federal gift tax (see p. 48). However, this tax does not apply to the owner's spouse, who benefits from an "unlimited marital deduction" with respect to gift tax. This tax can be avoided altogether if the joint ownership (in a bank or brokerage account, for example) is initially established for less than $10,000 and is periodically increased at a rate not exceeding $10,000 each year, because gifts of less than $10,000 annually are not subject to federal gift tax.

At the time of the original owner's death, anything in joint ownership with a nonspouse will be fully subject to federal estate tax except to the extent that the executor can prove that the surviving joint owner contributed to its acquisition or improvement (see p. 161).

A further disadvantage of joint ownership is that on the death of one owner, the surviving joint owner may receive a stepped-up basis of only 50 percent of the asset rather than the 100 percent had the asset been transferred by probate, through a trust, or through a transfer-on-death (TOD) designation.

In view of these limitations, the owner should, before selecting joint ownership for purposes of probate avoidance, carefully assess the issue of flexibility and control as well as the stability of his marriage and his relationship with any other prospective joint owners. Generally speaking, all its shortcomings make joint ownership a less-than-optimal plan for avoiding probate.

PAY-ON-DEATH ACCOUNTS

Pay-on-death accounts, offered by banks, savings and loan associations, and credit unions, constitute one of the simplest means of keeping money out of probate. One can add a POD designation to any new or existing account—checking, savings, or certificate of deposit—by adding to the signature card the names of one or more POD beneficiaries. The bank may ask for some additional information—such as the beneficiaries' date of birth or mailing address—but the beneficiaries need do nothing else. There is no charge for this procedure.

During the owner's lifetime, the POD beneficiaries have no rights to the account—and the owner pays taxes on its earnings. But if he should need the money or simply change his mind about leaving it to the beneficiaries, he can spend the money, change or eliminate beneficiaries, or close the account.

Those who live in a non-community-property state and choose someone other than a spouse as a POD account beneficiary should inform the spouse. In these states surviving spouses who are dissatisfied with their inheritance may be able to claim a specified percentage (usually one-third) of the deceased's property—known as the "statutory share." But since most spouses receive more than the statutory of the estate, it is unlikely that a spouse will go to court over this. And in some states POD accounts are not subject to a spouse's claim.

Although there are few restrictions on the choice of beneficiaries, some issues warrant consideration. If a minor named as a POD beneficiary is still a minor and unmarried at the time of the owner's death and the account is worth more than a few thousand dollars, it is wise to arrange for an adult to manage the money. If this is not done, one of two consequences may occur: (1) if the amount is small—generally a few thousand dollars, depending on state law and bank practice—the bank may turn it over to the child or the child's parents; (2) if the amount is substantial, the parents must petition a court for the appointment of a guardian or conservator to receive and manage the money. (If the parents are both deceased, presumably a guardian will have been appointed.)

The delay and expense of a court proceeding can be avoided by naming, on the POD form, an adult as custodian for the child under the Uniform Transfer to Minors Act (see p. 43).

More than one POD beneficiary can be named on an account if they are listed on the account registration. Unless otherwise specified, each will inherit an equal share of the balance, but state law governs this. An alternative is to establish separate POD accounts for each intended beneficiary.

It is not possible to name an alternate beneficiary—that is, someone to inherit the account should the first choice not survive the owner. It is widely believed that if three beneficiaries are listed and Number 1 predeceases the account owner, then Number 2 inherits Number 1's share as well as his own. But in fact the balance will be divided equally among the surviving beneficiaries. If this is not acceptable to the owner, he should immediately add a new beneficiary on the death of Number 1.

There are two further advantages to POD accounts. If the account restricts withdrawals before a specified date—a five-year certificate of deposit, for example—the early-withdrawal penalty will probably be waived. A second advantage deals with FDIC insurance of the account. Normally the FDIC insurance coverage of a maximum of $100,000 applies only the original owner's account. But if the POD beneficiary is a close relative—a spouse, grandchild, sibling, or parent—the FDIC coverage will be extended to the account after it passes to the beneficiary.

Despite their efficiency and economy, there are several disadvantages to POD accounts. Because their use is limited to bank products, they almost invariably pay a lower yield than other investments. Depending on the state of the economy and the stock market, you may prefer a Transfer-on-Death (TOD) account, which is usable for securities and just as simple to set up (see p. 42).

Some types of bank accounts cannot be converted automatically to POD accounts. If, for example, the account specifies "right of survivorship," a joint owner can name a beneficiary, but the survivor retains the right to eliminate or change the beneficiary. On the other hand, if the owners live in a community-property state, one half of the joint account belongs to each and each can designate a POD beneficiary for that half of the account balance.

Another disadvantage of the POD account is that the owner may not impose any conditions that the beneficiary must meet before receiving the money, a limitation that does not apply to a revocable living trust (see p. 44). But if this limitation is irrelevant, the POD is a far less expensive way of avoiding probate.

TOTTEN TRUSTS

POD accounts carry various designations in different states. A bank may respond to a POD request with a form authorizing the creation of something called a Totten trust account—essentially a POD account and similar to it in all respects. The name is derived from a New York case (*In re Totten*) that authorizes a person to open an account for another person—the beneficiary. The beneficiary has no right to the account funds until the original owner/trustee dies. After this decision, many states, adopting the concept of the Totten trust, enacted statutes authorizing POD accounts. Except for the terminology, the Totten trust account is essentially identical to the POD account.

TRANSFER-ON-DEATH
SECURITIES REGISTRATION

Transfer-on-death (TOD) securities registration, similar to the POD account, is used for stocks and bonds held in a brokerage account. It is set up by naming a beneficiary on the account preceded by the phrase "Transfer on death to . . ." The TOD beneficiary has no right to the assets in the account until the death of the owner, who can change or eliminate the beneficiary at any time. If authorized by the brokerage firm, the TOD account can name multiple beneficiaries as well as alternate beneficiaries.

Although it is possible to convert to TOD status individual stocks held by the owner, the process is so laborious that the owner is likely to be prompted to keep his investments in a broker's "street account" rather than in a safe deposit box. This means that when income tax is due, the broker will send the owner a comprehensive Form 1099 covering all transactions. It also frees the owner from having to find a security certificate and mail it to his broker each time a sale is made.

TABLE 3.1
Features of POD, Totten Trust, and TOD Accounts

	POD and Totten Trust Accounts	TOD Security Registration
Availability	Authorized by law in all states	Authorized by law in 47 states[1]
Cost to establish	None	Some brokers charge a fee
Multiple beneficiaries permitted	Yes[2]	Yes[2]
Alternative beneficiaries permitted	No[3]	Yes[4]
Revocable during owner's lifetime	Yes	Yes
Accessible by owner's creditors during his lifetime	Yes	Yes
Accessible by beneficiaries' creditors during owner's lifetime	No	No

---

TABLE 3.1
Features of POD, Totten Trust, and TOD Accounts (continued)

	POD and Totten Trust Accounts	TOD Security Registration
Designation by owner subject to federal gift tax	No	No
During owner's lifetime income from account/security remains taxable to owner	Yes	Yes
Upon owner's death account/ security included in owner's gross estate for federal estate tax purposes	Yes	Yes
Upon owner's death, surviving beneficiary gets stepped-up tax basis for capital gains tax purposes	N/A	Yes

[1] Provisions of the Uniform Transfer-on-Death Securities Registration Act have not been adopted in New York, North Carolina, and Texas.

[2] If multiple beneficiaries are named, each will share equally unless the owner specifies otherwise.

[3] If owner lists multiple beneficiaries, the bank will not consider the list to be a ranking in order of preference. Instead, the surviving beneficiaries will share equally.

[4] Subject to broker's policy, owner can name alternate beneficiaries for corporate securities but not for government bonds and notes.

CUSTODIAL ACCOUNTS

Some individuals set aside, in the form of bank accounts, certificates of deposit, or securities, a "nest egg" for their minor children, grandchildren, or others to be used for college tuition or other purposes.

If the asset remains solely in the owner's name, he pays taxes on its yield—presumably at a higher rate than the child would pay. On the other hand, if he gifts the asset to the child, the donor relinquishes all control over it.

A preferable arrangement is to establish for the minor a custodial account under the Uniform Gifts to Minors Act or the Uniform Transfer to Minors Act—one of which laws has been adopted by every state. Under this arrangement, the first $1,400 (for the year 2001) of the asset's earnings are taxed at the minor's (presumably lower) rate and the balance at the parents' rate until the child reaches age 14, at which time the entire yield is taxed at the child's rate.

Both principal and interest from a custodial account may be used by the custodian for *discretionary* expenses for the child, such as music lessons or orthodontia, but not for ordinary expenses such as food and clothing.

The disadvantage of a custodial account is that the child becomes entitled to the money on reaching age 18 (or, in some states, 21). Thus money intended for use as college tuition may be spent by the child for less worthwhile purposes.

The original donor may find it useful to name someone else as the custodian because if the owner should die before the account matures, its balance is included in his gross estate and hence may be taxable under the federal estate tax.

THE REVOCABLE LIVING TRUST

A probate-avoidance device that is far more flexible than joint ownership and has a number of advantages over a will is the revocable living trust, which is coming into wider use as increasing numbers of people recognize its usefulness.

The revocable living trust is a legal entity ("The Roger J. Smith Trust") into which the owner can transfer assets in any amount and of any kind: real estate, antiques, motor vehicles, boats, bank accounts, securities, and so on. Because the assets thus transferred legally belong to the trust and not to the owner, they are not probatable, but the owner, whether or not he serves as trustee, has full lifetime control over them; that is, they can be removed from the trust or sold or given away, new assets can be added, and the owner has full use of any earnings or growth. Although the owner can serve as the trustee (or as cotrustee with a spouse or another person or entity), a successor trustee is usually named in the trust to assume management of the trust assets should the original trustee lose interest, become disabled, or die.

The basic living trust document—known as the trust agreement—functions in many respects like a will, but it is far more flexible. Like a will, it can name beneficiaries, but it can also specify conditions that are harder to achieve under a will. If, for example, a will leaves assets to a child who reaches the age of 18 at the time of the owner's death, the child automatically inherits them, even though the child may be too immature to use them wisely. A living trust, on the other hand, can specify that the child cannot receive the assets until a later age. Although it is possible for a will to make such a trust provision, it would require probate of the estate and court supervision of the terms of the will-created trust.

In addition to designating the beneficiaries and specifying how and when the trust assets are to be distributed, the trust agreement should specify the rate of compensation (if any) of the trustees, the duration of the trust, and any other conditions governing the management, investment, and distribution of the trust's assets.

Like a will, the trust agreement can be revised at any time during the owner's lifetime, and provision can be made in the owner's will that any assets not in the trust be "poured over" into the trust on the owner's death. Similarly, the trust can be named as beneficiary of the owner's life insurance, IRA, Keogh, SEP, and 401K accounts, and any other contractual benefits.

The trust is managed by a trustee (or cotrustees) who are fully responsible for safeguarding the trust assets, investing them prudently so as to maximize their yield, and distributing or applying them in compliance with instructions in the trust. The owner can be the initial trustee or can serve as a cotrustee with a spouse or with anyone else named in the trust agreement. Upon the owner's resignation, disability, or death, control of the trust assets passes to the successor trustee, who must distribute them to the trust's beneficiaries according to the terms of the trust agreement. Some persons owning large or complicated estates designate a bank or a trust company as trustee or successor trustee, but the fees that institutional trustees charge for this service may be considerable and may bear no relationship to the services performed.

Although the revocable living trust is thoroughly effective for avoiding probate, it offers no protection against creditors. If, for example, an automobile accident in which the owner is found negligent results in a judgment that exceeds the owner's liability insurance coverage, assets owned by the trust can be attached to satisfy the excess damages. And, although some states prohibit creditors from making claims against trust-held assets, a trust does not offer the "limited liability" that corporate shareholders enjoy.

The basic revocable living trust does not provide a shelter against either income tax or federal estate tax. The owner remains responsible for taxes on whatever income the trust assets produce and, on his death, their entire value may be subject to federal estate tax. It is possible, however, to use a revocable living trust to establish a "credit shelter trust" or "bypass trust."

Using this tactic, married couples who own an estate of up to $1,350,000 can shield the assets entirely from the federal estate tax, which is applicable only to estates exceeding $675,000[1] (see Chapter 9). The first $675,000[1] is left in a trust for the children or other beneficiaries, and the balance passes to the survivor's spouse. The surviving spouse can receive all income from the trust, but the trust's principal will pass to the trust-designated beneficiaries on the death of the second spouse.

Because a revocable living trust is a sophisticated estate-planning tool, it should be prepared by a lawyer experienced in estate planning. The owner, in a face-to-face meeting, can custom-tailor the trust and related documents to achieve his individual goals. This should not cost more than five to 10 hours of a lawyer's time and will involve lawyer's fees currently ranging from $1,000 to $2,000.

Although there are on the market several do-it-yourself books and forms for living trust preparation, these one-size-fits-all documents are unlikely to embody the very specific terms that the owner may require. And although companies that offer living trust preparation have proliferated in recent years, they have been the subject of widespread consumer complaints on grounds of overcharging, misrepresentation, and failure to provide adequately all the services promised.

THE IRREVOCABLE LIVING TRUST

Like the revocable living trust, the irrevocable living trust not only avoids probate but, in addition, it offers the owner the opportunity of reducing both current income tax and future death taxes.

As the term "irrevocable" implies, however, this form of trust requires the owner to relinquish forever the trust assets, all personal use of the income they produce, and all control over them. This makes the irrevocable trust attractive only to individuals of very substantial means.

Although it is possible for the owner to serve as trustee of an irrevocable trust, most owners appoint a bank or trust company, because this guarantees that the owner will not use the trust proceeds for personal benefit.

---

[1] The estate tax exclusion amount, which is $675,000 for deaths during 2000 and 2001, is indexed for inflation up to 2006, at which time it reaches $1 million (see Table 9.2, p.164).

Income taxes on the earnings of an irrevocable trust are payable by the trust itself or by the trust's beneficiaries (presumably at a lower rate than the owner's) and there are no inheritance or estate taxes levied. Establishment of the trust will subject the owner to gift tax if the assets initially transferred to the trust amount to more than $10,000 per beneficiary—or $20,000 if the donor's spouse consents to the transfer. But, as in the case of the revocable living trust, the irrevocable trust can be established initially in a lower amount and increased periodically with amounts too low to incur any gift tax.

As you can see, the irrevocable living trust is useful for rich individuals who wish to reduce income and estate taxes and who do not need the assets that they part with. For most individuals it is not practical, because they cannot with certainty foretell their own financial needs.

CHARITABLE GIFTS

Although certain charitable gifts are tax-deductible at any time during the owner's life, and although a will may make provisions for further gifts, some philanthropic organizations offer donors a lifetime income in return for a large gift. This provides the donor not only with a substantial tax deduction but also with a source of income that is guaranteed, although it is not protected against inflation.

One popular type of charitable gift—of particular interest to those who have no immediate family to whom they wish to leave their estate—is the "charitable remainder trust." Under this arrangement, the donor can use the income produced by the trust, but the trust's assets pass, on the donor's death, to the charity designated in the trust.

INCORPORATION

One of the most difficult problems confronting an executor is the disposition of the deceased's sole proprietorship, limited liability company, or partnership business interests, whether it be an accounting practice, a hardware store, or any other business. Not only must a decision be made as to whether to liquidate the business or sell it as a going concern, but there is likely to be conflict about this decision among the beneficiaries.

One way to simplify the problem is to recommend that the owner incorporate the business. Once this is done, the corporate shares can be bequeathed to the beneficiaries and the decision as to what to do with the business is made by majority vote of the shareholders.

There may be other advantages to incorporation, but it is also possible that there are disadvantages that make it undesirable or impractical. (A lawyer experienced in estate planning can explain both.) Nevertheless, the corporate form of ownership should be considered as one way of simplifying the later valuation, distribution, and settlement of the probate estate.

"GIFTING OFF" ASSETS

In order to reduce their estate below the minimum limit of the federal estate tax, some people simply give away assets to beneficiaries before they die. This has the further effect of reducing their tax liability for income generated by such assets. And, perhaps more important, it permits the donor to enjoy the gratitude of the recipients while he is still alive.

But there are two possible disadvantages to this plan. To begin with, gifts of more than $10,000 (or $20,000 with consent of the donor's spouse) are subject to federal gift tax. In addition, the recipient of a gift of assets must, when they are sold, use as a tax basis what they originally cost the donor, and not the 100 percent stepped-up tax basis had the gift been made via probate, through a revocable living trust, or by use or a transfer-on-death beneficiary designation. Hence, if gifted securities, for example, have appreciated substantially, the recipient will be burdened with a significant capital gains tax when the securities are sold. If, on the other hand, the securities are bequeathed by will or transferred at death via a revocable living trust or transfer-on-death designation where allowed, their tax basis is "stepped up" to their value as of the date of the testator/grantor's death.

Table 3.2 summarizes the various strategies for reducing the value of the probate estate.

THE VALUE OF PRE-DEATH PLANNING

If the testator adopts some of the suggestions offered in this chapter, you will have accomplished two important goals. First, you will have reassured the testator that he has done a great deal to protect the interests of the survivors. Second, you will have simplified—if not, in fact, entirely eliminated—your own role as executor.

TABLE 3.2
Legal Consequences of Various Forms of Ownership

Form of Ownership	Subject to		Control During Your Lifetime	Bequeath-able by Will	Subject to Creditors' Claims		Availability to Beneficiaries
	Probate	Federal Estate Tax			Before Death	After Death	
Asset solely owned	Yes	All	Full	Yes	Yes	Yes	Delayed
Asset owned jointly with spouse	No[1]	One-half	Divided	No[1]	Yes	No[2]	Immediate[1]
Asset owned jointly with others	No[1]	All[3]	Divided	No[1]	Yes	No[1]	Immediate[1]
Assets in POD bank account	No	All	Full	No	Yes	No	Immediate
Assets in TOD securities account	No	All	Full	No	Yes	No	Immediate
Assets in custodial account for minors	No	None[4]	None[4]	No	No	No	Immediate
Life insurance owned by insured	No[6]	All	Full	No[6]	No	No[6]	Immediate
Life insurance owned by other than insured	No[6]	None[8]	None	No	No	No[6]	Immediate

Life insurance payable to deceased's estate	Yes	All	Full	Yes	Yes[7]	Yes	Delayed
Assets in a revocable living trust	No	All	Full	No	Yes	Perhaps[9]	Immediate[5]
Assets in an irrevocable living trust	No	None	None	No	No	No	Immediate[5]

[1] Provided that the joint owner survives

[2] Unless debt was incurred by both joint owners.

[3] Except to the extent your estate can prove that a surviving joint owner contributed to the acquisition or improvement of the property.

[4] Unless you are a custodian as well as a donor.

[5] Subject, however, to all of the terms of the trust, which may include a provision postponing distribution of the property.

[6] Provided that a beneficiary designated in the insurance policy survives. Otherwise the proceeds become a part of the probate estate.

[7] Limited to the cash surrender value of the policy.

[8] Unless the policy is assigned to another within three years of the date of death.

[9] Several states expose revocable trust assets to creditors' claims.

Part II

FIRST THINGS FIRST

4

WILLS, ANATOMIC GIFTS, AND FUNERALS

What you do immediately after a death depends, of course, on your relationship with the deceased. If you are a close relative, you will undoubtedly be involved in notifying family and friends, in making funeral arrangements, and in all the other details that confront survivors during the first few days. But even if you are only a close friend, the deceased's family may need your active participation, especially if they are overwhelmed with grief. In addition, because, as the nominated executor, you may later be responsible for payment of the funeral and burial or cremation expenses, you should, if possible, take an active role even though you have no official capacity until the court has appointed you and issued your letters of authority.

This chapter deals with the various steps that must be taken soon after death occurs. You can skip it only if you are fairly sure that they are being dealt with competently by others.

LOCATING THE WILL

Since you have been nominated executor, the chances are good that you know where the original will is located. If not, you might inquire of the county probate court, where many testators file their wills for safekeeping. Before the death, the probate court can release the original to anyone producing the receipt issued for the

Figure 4.1

STATE OF MICHIGAN PROBATE COURT COUNTY OF	PETITION AND ORDER TO OPEN SAFE DEPOSIT BOX TO LOCATE WILL OR BURIAL DEED	FILE NO.

Estate of _____

> ### PETITION

1. I am an interested person as _____ of decedent, who
   Heir, devisee, etc.

   died _____ .
   Date

2. _____ as lessor, leased to
   Name of bank, trust company, or safe deposit company

   decedent, alone or jointly, safe deposit box number _____ , located

   at _____ in _____ in this county, and
   Branch   *City or township*

   the safe deposit box may contain decedent's will or a deed to a burial plot
   in which the decedent is to be interred.

3. I REQUEST that this court issue an order directing the lessor to permit
   _____ to examine the contents of the safe
   Name

   deposit box in the presence of an officer or other authorized employee of
   lessor for the purpose of locating and removing a will and deed to a
   burial plot only.

I declare under the penalties of perjury that this petition has been examined
by me and that its contents are true to the best of my information, knowledge, and belief.

_____
Date

_____	_____
Attorney signature	*Petitioner signature*
_____	_____
Name (type or print) *Bar no.*	*Name (type or print)* *Bar no.*
_____	_____
Address	*Address*
_____	_____
City, state, zip *Telephone no.*	*City, state, zip* *Telephone no.*

Figure 4.1 *(continued)*

ORDER

IT IS ORDERED:

4. The above petition is granted and the lessor is ordered to permit _____ to examine the above described safe deposit box in the presence of an officer or other authorized employee of the lessor. Only a will of the decedent and a deed to a burial plot shall be removed from the box and shall be delivered by the above named person to the probate register or deputy register of this court.

5. At the time of the opening of the safe deposit box, all persons in attendance shall execute a written statement certifying whether a will or deed to a burial plot was found and that no other items were removed from the safe deposit box. The person named above shall file that written statement with the probate register or deputy register of this court within 7 days of opening the box.

Date	*Judge*	*Bar no.*

Do not write below this line - For court use only

will. After the death, the court will provide anyone with copies but must retain the original.

Alternatively, it is possible that the original will can be found in the office of the deceased's lawyer who prepared it. You might also check the deceased's safe deposit box, although getting immediate access to the box may present some difficulties. If you cannot open the box, you may petition the court for an immediate order authorizing you to do so (see Figure 4.1).

If you have a photocopy but can't find the original, check your state law governing the procedure for proving lost wills. If you can produce witnesses to establish that the original was indeed signed by the testator, some states permit a copy to be admitted in place of the original.

If you have neither the original nor a copy, and if you believe that the deceased signed a will, consider publishing a notice in the newsletter of the local bar association or estate planning council (see Figure 4.2).

Figure 4.2

NOTICE SEEKING WILL

WANTED: INFORMATION ABOUT WILL. Survivors are seeking an original, a copy, or information regarding the will of John J. Jones, formerly of 101 Capitol Ave., Lansing, MI, who died January 1, 2001. Persons having information are asked to contact Fred F. Fiduciary, Executor of the Jones Estate, 201 Main St., Lansing, MI 48909, telephone (517) 123-4567. Collect calls accepted.

Although novels and detective stories may have left you with the impression that an urgent search for the will immediately after the testator's death is a mark of villainous greed, the fact is that the will should be located and read promptly. Not only will it disclose your nomination as executor, but it may contain provisions—about funeral and burial arrangements, for example, or anatomic gifts—that require immediate action since they will be frustrated if there is any delay in collecting the body or harvesting the organs. In addition, a will is likely to nominate guardians of minor children orphaned by the death.

BODY DISPOSAL AND FUNERAL RITES

Unless you are a family member, you, as the executor, have no direct role in or responsibility for arranging the funeral and burial (or cremation). But if probate proceedings are under way and the funeral director files a creditor's claim against the estate, you will become involved. If the probate court determines that the funeral director sold too elaborate a funeral to a family of limited means, or that the family was overcharged or defrauded, it can order that the bill be reduced—or not paid at all—even if the contract was cosigned by a survivor. Hence, even though others may be making the arrangements, you should, if possible, be aware of them.

The first task facing the survivors—planning for the funeral ritual and disposal of the body—is almost inevitably painful and difficult. Grief, inexperience, and the pressure of time may combine to impair their judgment and lead to a number of decisions they might otherwise not make.

Grief, especially if it is compounded with guilt and remorse—the feeling that "now it's too late" to do for the deceased all that they might have done—can cause them to compensate for their earlier failings, real or imagined, by overspending for a needlessly elaborate funeral.

Inexperience—because a death in the family is, after all, a very infrequent event—can result in mistakes in buying funeral and burial goods and services that would not be made in buying something equally expensive but more familiar.

Time pressure, often exerted by a hospital, nursing home, or morgue in its eagerness to get rid of the body, can lead survivors into making hasty arrangements with the first funeral home that comes to mind without considering alternative arrangements that might be less expensive or more satisfactory.

The stress that survivors feel and the mistakes that result from it are to some extent unavoidable, but they can be reduced to a minimum if two basic principles are followed. First, the survivors should not allow themselves to be pressured into hasty decisions. Second, no matter who takes on the major responsibility, other relatives or close family friends should be involved in the planning. Decisions arrived at jointly are likely to be more objective and more rational and—perhaps more important—they can avert the arguments and long-term alienation among family members that often stem from disagreements over what should or should not have been done.

RESISTING THE PRESSURES

If the death has occurred in a hospital or a nursing home, that institution may show indecent haste in urging the removal of the body. Indeed, the same telephone call that informed survivors of the death may have included a request that survivors "make arrangements" before the end of the day.

This urgency is understandable from the institution's point of view. Bodies, if they are awaiting autopsy or if they are to remain in an enbalmable condition, must be refrigerated, and most hospitals, especially those that do autopsies for the county medical examiner as well as on their own patients, suffer a chronic shortage of refrigerator space. And many nursing homes have no facilities whatever for refrigerating the body.

But from the survivors' point of view, this urgency is important only if the deceased left his or her body or specific organs as an anatomic gift or if they are making the gift themselves on behalf of the deceased (see p. 61). In such circumstances, time is of the essence, because the donated organs must be harvested and preserved within a few hours of death, or the entire body must be promptly transported to the donee.

In the absence of an anatomic gift, however, there is no reason to feel pressed for time, because the institution is prohibited by law from disposing of the body without the consent of the next of kin. Keeping the body for a reasonable length of time may inconvenience the institution, but yielding to pressure and, as a result, making arrangements that have not been thought out and discussed with others, is a worse alternative.

Occasionally, nursing home or hospital personnel will suggest the name of a funeral home that can remove the body promptly. Although such a suggestion may be well intentioned, survivors would not be paranoid if they suspected a financial arrangement between the funeral home and the "helpful" employee. In most cases, they would do better to make their own choice.

In years past, it was not uncommon for hospital personnel to call a favored funeral home and instruct it to pick up the body without any authorization from the survivors—on the pretext that it had to be embalmed. This practice has presumably disappeared, because it is now strictly illegal. A funeral director who takes possession of a body or embalms or cremates it without authorization from the next of kin, or who refuses to release the body to the next of kin, faces immediate loss of license as well as a possible lawsuit brought by the survivors.

DEATH AT HOME

If a death occurs in a hospital or nursing home, the death certificate (which must be executed before the body can be removed to a funeral home) can be signed either by the deceased's attending physician or by any physician on the staff of the institution. If the death occurs at home, however, the death certificate must be signed by the deceased's physician or by the county medical examiner (sometimes called the coroner).

In two sets of circumstances, involvement of the medical examiner is required by law. First, he or she must be notified if the deceased was not under the care of a physician. (The definition of "under the care of a physician" varies from state to state; in some it means having been seen by a physician during the 48 hours preceding death; in others the time limit is two weeks or more.) In most such situations the death is likely to have been sudden and the cause unclear. Second, the medical examiner must be notified of any death resulting from violence—not only possible suicide or homicide but also accidents of all kinds. In some states the medical examiner may waive the examination, but the death should always be reported by telephone to the examiner's office.

SOME LEGAL CONSTRAINTS

Before making any plans or decisions, you need to be aware of state laws that govern anatomic gifts and autopsies and that specify who has the final say about funeral arrangements, disposition of the body, and responsibility for the funeral bill. Although some of these laws are often violated and seldom enforced, a general understanding of them can help you avoid problems.

ANATOMIC GIFTS

Under the Uniform Anatomical Gift Act, currently the law in all states, any gifts of organs or of the entire body properly made in writing by the deceased must be honored by the survivors. After the donor's death, the person in possession of the gift document—usually a donor card (see Figure 4.3) but sometimes a will—is legally obligated to carry out the instructions it contains. However, the deceased's intent may be frustrated, deliberately or otherwise, by several circumstances.

To begin with, unless the body or any donated organs are in medically usable condition, the gift will not be accepted. Although the gift may be rendered unusable by disease or mutilation, the more common problem is delay: the body or organs must be received by the donee within a very few hours of death. If an anatomical gift is made by means of a will, and if the will is not found or read until a day or two after the death, neither the body

Figure 4.3

UNIFORM DONOR CARD

OF _____
Print or type name of donor

In the hope that I may help others, I hereby make this anatomic gift, if medically acceptable, to take effect upon my death. The words and marks below indicate my desires.

I give: (a) _____ any needed organs or parts
   (b) _____ only the following organs or parts

_____
Specify the organ(s) or part(s)

for the purposes of transplantation, therapy, medical research or education;
   (c) _____ my body, for anatomic study if needed.

Limitations or special wishes, if any: _____
_____

Signed by the donor and the following two witnesses in the presence of each other:

_____   _____
  Signature of Donor   *Date of Birth of Donor*

_____   _____
  Date Signed   *City & State*

_____   _____
  Date Signed   *Witness*

This is a legal document under the Uniform Anatomical Gift Act or similar laws.

For further information consult your physician or

National Kidney Foundation Inc.
1 Park Avenue, New York, NY 10016

---

nor the organs will be medically usable and the named donee is almost certain to reject the intended gift.

The gift of a body or its organs may also be refused if, at the time it is offered, there is an adequate supply or if transportation from the place of death to the donee institution proves to be impractical or too expensive. The donee always has the right to decline a gift for any reason—or for no reason at all. On the other hand, the donee has the right to accept the gift and, if it is already well supplied, to divert it to another institution that has a greater need for it. Thus, the donor cannot be certain that the ultimate recipient will be the institution he originally designated.

In all such situations, the survivors, having made good faith efforts to comply with the deceased's wishes, are free to choose any alternative method of body disposal.

Even if the anatomic gift is made through a properly witnessed donor card, it may be frustrated by a reluctant survivor who conceals or destroys the card, refuses to sign the consent form that most institutional donees require, or fails to notify the designated donee. Although destruction of the donor card is a clear violation of the law, it is unlikely to result in court action, because the monetary value of the gift is too low to induce the prospective donee to file suit.

AUTOPSIES

In all cases of violent death, and in most cases of death under unknown or unusual circumstances, an autopsy to determine the cause of death is required by law. In such situations there is nothing that survivors can do except modify whatever arrangements they have made to allow time for the autopsy to be completed.

Often, however, even when the cause of death is known, the attending physician or the hospital will ask permission of the survivors to perform an autopsy in order to learn more about the deceased's condition at the time of death or about the disease from which the patient died. There is no charge for this service.

Although the prospect of having the deceased's body surgically invaded and the organs removed and examined may be repugnant, survivors should carefully consider the possible benefits to society or to themselves personally. In addition to its usefulness to physicians, an autopsy can offer survivors considerable comfort if the results indicate that a death that seemed sudden and inexplicable was, in fact, inevitable within days or weeks of its occurrence. Moreover, an autopsy may provide blood relatives with medical information that is relevant to their own health or longevity.

Autopsies do not, of course, preclude an open-casket funeral. Cosmetic restoration by the funeral director can effectively conceal any indications that an autopsy has been performed.

THE DECEASED'S WISHES

Aside from making an anatomic gift, the only other legally binding way in which a person can specify the disposition of his or her body is through a will. (Wishes expressed in a letter of instruction [see p. 25] or in any other informal way, orally or in writing, have no legal standing.) But the instructions specified in a will are not always carried out—either because the survivors ignore the will, or because the will has not been discovered or read before the body disposal has taken place, or because the survivors go to court to have the instructions set aside as unreasonable or unduly burdensome.

The deceased may, of course, have negotiated a pre-need contract with a funeral home, specifying the kind of funeral and body disposal desired, stipulating the price to be paid, and depositing a sum of money to pay for it. But even legal contracts of this kind have been successfully contested by survivors claiming that the money was more urgently needed for their own welfare.

WHO HAS THE RIGHT TO DECIDE?

One major problem, experienced by survivors and funeral directors alike, stems from uncertainty as to who has the final say on all details of the ritual service and the disposal of the body. Such issues as cremation versus burial, or open versus closed casket, can generate not only heated arguments among the survivors at the time of death but also, occasionally, lifelong enmities within the family. Funeral directors, for their part, complain that often, after they have set up painstakingly detailed arrangements with one member of the family, another arrives to countermand that person in favor of something entirely different.

Family conflicts of this kind often stem from intergenerational differences. On the death of a young man, for example, his widow may prefer a simple secular service followed by cremation, because both she and her husband had long ago abandoned formal religious observances. The husband's parents, on the other hand, may insist on an elaborate religious service, a luxurious casket, grave burial, and an expensive grave marker—even though they have neither the intention nor the ability to pay the funeral and burial costs, which may have to come out of a pitifully small estate left to the widow.

Actually the laws of your state specify, in priority sequence, the persons who have the right to make decisions about funeral and burial arrangements. But, as we shall see, these laws are relatively easy to evade and difficult to enforce.

In general, the following persons, in order of precedence, have the right to decide on all arrangements: the surviving spouse (if not estranged), an adult child, a parent, an adult sibling, a guardian of the deceased, or "any other person authorized or obligated to dispose of the body"—presumably a medical examiner or the administrator of a hospital or nursing home. But although the order of priority is clear, and although it may be useful to cite in an attempt to settle family disagreements, it rarely becomes the subject of a lawsuit—in part because disposition of the body usually must take place before court action is feasible, and because few judges will order a body exhumed so that it can undergo an alternative method of disposal or be buried in a different place.

WHO PAYS THE FUNERAL BILL?

Under state law, all "reasonable" funeral expenses are chargeable against the estate of the deceased, even if the arrangements are made by a surviving relative other than the executor. This is why you should play as active a role as possible in the decision. A relative who makes any payment for funeral services is entitled to reimbursement from the estate.

Often, however, there may be no estate, or it may be too small to cover the funeral bill, or the funeral director may have no idea of the financial situation of the deceased or the survivors. In such cases, the funeral director is likely to require the person making the arrangements to cosign for the bill or to guarantee payment should the estate prove unable to pay. For this reason, this person should scrutinize carefully all papers relating to funeral arrangements before signing them. In some cases, these papers authorize certain services; in others, they signify acceptance of responsibility for the bill. Anyone who accepts such responsibility will be legally responsible for the entire bill or for whatever part of it the estate is unable or unwilling to pay.

One way of reducing the direct charges against the estate (or against the cosigner or guarantor) is to sign over to the funeral director any Social Security death benefits or veteran's death benefits to which the deceased is entitled (see p. 80). Taken together, these may cover the funeral director's basic costs and persuade him that cosigning is unnecessary. In addition, the funeral director rather than the executor or another survivor will have to do the paper-work involved in applying for these benefits and endure the delay until they are paid. Most funeral directors are quite willing to do this, because it assures them of at least some payment.

Under the law, the funeral director enjoys a preferred status among the estate's creditors; his bill must be paid in full before any other debts except administration expenses (court costs, attorney fees, and executor's fees and expenses) and taxes are paid. In return for this preferred status, the funeral director is expected to behave more ethically and more professionally toward his customers than most other suppliers of consumer goods and services, and the courts have frequently disapproved or reduced funeral bills that seemed exorbitant—not merely in absolute terms but in relation to the size of the estate or the income level of the surviving family. If a dis-traught widow is exploited by an unethical funeral director, or even if the funeral director permits her to order an excessively expensive funeral, she—or you as the executor—may seek relief in the courts. Many, if not most, funeral directors are aware of this and govern their behavior accordingly.

WHOSE FUNERAL IS IT?

As our review of the legal situation indicates, the law is both spe-cific and enforceable with respect to autopsies in certain cases and with respect to funeral and burial expenses. Most of the other legal provisions—those governing anatomic gifts, compliance with funeral and burial instructions expressed in the will, the standing and priority of persons making funeral decisions, and the validity of pre-need contracts—can often be disregarded, contested, or cir-cumvented. Thus, although the survivors may wish to honor the deceased by carrying out his or her wishes, they can feel reasonably comfortable about disregarding them if they seem capricious, unduly burdensome, or otherwise unreasonable.

Fundamentally, a funeral is for the benefit not of the deceased but of the survivors. It should, within the financial limits of the deceased's estate, be as satisfying as possible to all of them—emo-tionally, esthetically, and socially. A young widow may be entirely justified in disregarding the expensive preferences of her in-laws if satisfying them would threaten the future welfare of herself and her children. On the other hand, some survivors may feel that disregarding or rejecting a close relative's strong preferences is unwise if it jeopardizes a lifelong relationship.

For all these reasons, even though the responsibility for choice of arrangements and for payment of their cost is clearly specified by law, the most satisfactory funeral arrangements usually represent a compromise among the preferences of various family members. To achieve this compromise, the best plan is to arrange a meeting (or a long-distance conference call) among the survivors in the hope of achieving some consensus on the following alternatives.

SOME BASIC ALTERNATIVES

As they begin formulating specific funeral arrangements, survivors need to bear in mind that two separate procedures are involved: a ritual service of some sort and the physical disposal of the body. Although these procedures are not entirely independent of one another—for example, an anatomical gift of an entire body precludes a casket service—they can be put together in a number of combinations. For this reason, they may require separate decisions.

In some situations, simply following the wishes of the deceased—whether or not they are legally binding—can relieve the survivors of all responsibility, or at least of the responsibility for disposal of the body. If, for example, a pre-need contract with a funeral home was negotiated by the deceased, and if this arrangement seems reasonable and appropriate, the survivors need merely set it in motion by notifying the funeral home that the death has occurred. In such circumstances, it is likely that the ritual service as well as the body-disposal method has been specified.

An anatomic gift of the entire body solves the problem of body disposal but not of the ritual service. If, however, the anatomic gift involves only one or more organs and not the entire body, the responsibility for both ritual service and body disposal remain.

One way to review and evaluate the available alternatives is to consult Table 4.1, which presents the entire array of rituals and disposal methods. The table is necessarily simplified, and it is not intended as a guide to detailed funeral arrangements, but a thoughtful reading of it can (1) make survivors aware of some alternatives they may not have considered; (2) provide a general notion of the procedures involved in—and the relative costs of—the various alternatives; and thus (3) protect them against suggestions offered by a possibly greedy or unethical funeral director.

Although Table 4.1 emphasizes costs, both the ritual service and the disposal of the body have not only economic consequences for the survivors but also profound social and psychological significance. It is important, therefore, that decisions not be based on cost alone. If, for example, direct disposal with cremation appalls the survivors esthetically or threatens the religious beliefs of close kin, the fact that it is the cheapest method should not sway the decision. On the other hand, it may be irresponsible to spend on unessential funeral services money that could make a significant difference in the survivors' future standard of living.

The social and psychological significance of the various styles of ritual service, and of the several methods of body disposal, is such an individual and personal matter that little can be said about it in a book of this kind. Perhaps the most effective way to reach a satisfying compromise among the economic, psychological, and other considerations is for the survivors to answer collectively the following questions. Although the answers will be determined largely by their feelings, the economic implications will be inescapable.

A BODY-CENTERED OR A PERSON-CENTERED FUNERAL?

If the survivors focus on the body of the deceased, they will probably choose (as many Americans do) a service with an open casket, visitation and viewing of the body for one or two days, a cortege to the cemetery, a grave burial, and a highly visible grave marker. Because an open-casket service requires embalming and cosmetic restoration, an above-minimum-price casket, and a number of other goods and services provided by a funeral home (see Table 4.1), this is by far the most expensive form of funeral.

If, on the other hand, the survivors feel (as do an increasing number of Americans) that the body is less significant and that they want to focus on the individual's character and social relationships, they may prefer direct disposal by cremation and, perhaps, burial or scattering of the ashes, followed by a memorial service at a later date. With this choice, many of the most expensive components of the traditional funeral—embalming, cosmetic restoration, the casket, the use of a funeral home for visitation, the cemetery plot, the grave liner, opening and closing the grave, and the grave marker—are eliminated.

TABLE 4.1

Funeral Alternatives

Ritual	Body Disposal	Essential Costs*	Optional Costs*
Service with body present			
With casket open for viewing	Burial	1-10	11, 14, 15
	Cremation	1–4, 6–8, 12	9–11, 13–15
With closed casket	Burial	1, 3, 4,a 5–10	11, 14, 15
	Cremation	1, 3, 4,b 6–8, 12	9–11, 13–15
Graveside service only			
Closed casket	Burial	4, 5, 8–10	3, 11, 14, 15
Memorial service, body not present			
	Burial	c	14, 15
	Cremation	c	14, 15
	Body donationd	Nonee	14, 15

* Key to Costs

1. Transportation of body from place of death.
2. Embalming and cosmetic restoration.
3. Other professional services by funeral home staff.
4. Casket.
5. Vault or grave liner (not required by law but often required by cemeteries).
6. Viewing and/or visitation facilities at funeral home.
7. Chapel facilities at funeral home (or additional transportation charges to move body to house of worship).
8. Transportation of body to grave or crematory.
9. Cost of cemetery plot.
10. Opening and closing of grave.
11. Transportation of mourners by limousine to and from committal.
12. Crematory charge.
13. Columbarium charge for urn committal.
14. Clergy fee.
15. Classified obituary notices.

a A less expensive casket can be used, because it is not the center of attention and can be covered with flowers or a pall.

b Casket can be replaced by a much less expensive crematory container.

c One all-inclusive charge covers all costs of body disposal, but memorial service and claiming of death benefits remain responsibility of survivors.

d For research or teaching and eventual cremation.

e The body (in a sealed casket) or the cremated ashes may be returned for disposal by the survivors, but this is rarely done.

Although the cost differences between these two alternatives are obvious, the psychological differences are not. Some psychologists (and virtually all funeral directors) firmly believe that it is only after viewing the body that survivors accept the reality and finality of the death, and that such viewing actually facilitates the grieving process. And some of them believe that even young children should view the body.

Other psychologists (and many clergymen), however, argue the opposite point of view with equal conviction. They do not feel that viewing a highly cosmeticized corpse helps the survivors accept the death, and they feel that in some circumstances viewing the corpse may be a traumatic experience. They point out that concern for the physical body may divert attention from the quality of the deceased's relationships, accomplishments, and personality.

There are no scientific data to support either position, but it is doubtful that such data would change the survivors' convictions.

LARGELY PUBLIC OR LARGELY PRIVATE?

If the deceased was a public figure or simply a person with a vast array of friends and acquaintances, the survivors may feel obligated to give people an opportunity to mark the death, and this may require turning the funeral into a public event, complete with visitation and viewing, a large and elaborate ritual service, a cortege, and other features that the survivors themselves might prefer to avoid.

In such circumstances, compromises are, of course, possible. Even if the ritual service is likely to attract large numbers of people, there is no need for the casket to be open, and it is quite possible for the committal (whether by burial or cremation) to be restricted to members of the immediate family. It is also possible to keep the entire funeral simple and private, and to hold a larger, more public memorial service at a later date. In general, the more public the funeral, the more expensive it is likely to be.

In thinking about the funeral in relation to people outside the immediate family, it is useful to distinguish between people with whom the deceased was socially *involved* and those whom the survivors would like to *impress*. As we've noted, the social obligation to the deceased's friends is both real and largely unavoidable. On the other hand, some survivors arrange expensive and elaborate funerals merely to impress people in the community—people with whom the deceased may have had no relationship. A funeral, however, seems a rather futile occasion for keeping up with the Joneses.

CREMATION OR EARTH BURIAL?

Because the esthetic and philosophical aspects of cremation have been dealt with earlier, we shall restrict our discussion here to comparative costs. If the survivors bear in mind that cremation is simply a method of body disposal that can be used with any type of ritual service—from a simple pre- or postcremation memorial service to the most elaborate open-casket-with-visitation service—they will realize that its actual cost requires a careful comparison with earth burial (see Table 4.1).

Cremation would seem to be cheaper than earth burial because, although the ashes may be buried in a cemetery, this is not necessary. If no cemetery is used, there are no costs for a plot, a grave liner, a grave marker, or for opening and closing the grave. But this obvious saving will be reduced by the charges the crematorium makes for its services, and possibly by additional charges if the ashes are to be "inurned" and kept permanently in a columbarium—an urn repository usually operated by the crematorium.

Cremation can also be cheaper because it requires, instead of a casket, only an inexpensive corrugated cardboard container—but this saving will not be realized if an open-casket ritual service is chosen. Similarly, cremation does not require embalming or cosmetic restoration—but neither does earth burial with a closed casket or a graveside service.

It is likely that the cost difference between cremation and earth burial will increase as the price of cemetery plots continues to rise. At the time of this writing, however, the difference in cost between cremation and earth burial is not as great as many people believe, and the fact that cremation is chosen more often by people who are well-to-do suggests that the choice is frequently made on other than economic grounds.

OBTAINING THE CHOSEN SERVICES

Once the survivors have decided on the style of ritual service and the method of body disposal, they are ready to get in touch with one of the following organizations.

DIRECT-DISPOSAL FIRMS

Direct-disposal firms operate at present in only a very few states, largely because the funeral industry lobby has successfully opposed them in the others. These firms provide a minimal one-price service that includes removal of the body from the place of death and either burial (in a grave provided by the survivors) or cremation. The disposal is carried out so promptly that no embalming is required and, since there is no viewing, neither is cosmetic restoration. Survivors who use this service usually plan a memorial service some time after the death. They take responsibility, also, for applying for death benefits and for the incidental services (such as obituary publication) normally provided by the conventional funeral home.

Whether these firms' appeal is primarily to survivors seeking low-cost services or to those who take a person-centered rather than a body-centered approach to death is unclear, but the fact is that these firms are flourishing despite the persistent efforts of the funeral industry to place legislative or regulatory obstacles in their path.

If their state does not license direct-disposal firms, there is no reason why survivors should not ask for similar direct-disposal service from a conventional funeral home or a crematorium. Because the Federal Trade Commission rule requires funeral homes to maintain an itemized price list of their services, it is possible to order only those services that are necessary for prompt, direct disposal. There may be some resistance or downright refusals, but it is likely that at least one available funeral home in each area will quote a price for exactly what the survivors want.

MEMORIAL SOCIETIES

More widely available than direct-disposal firms are memorial societies, which originated more than 50 years ago as consumer cooperatives aimed specifically at reducing the high cost of funerals and providing their members with dignified funerals at minimal cost. Although, like direct-disposal firms, memorial societies have aroused the hostility of the funeral industry, that opposition has not been effective enough to prevent the societies' spread, and today almost 200 such societies exist throughout the United States and Canada.

All memorial societies, whether religiously affiliated or secular, are devoted to public service and are operated almost entirely by volunteers, but they differ somewhat in the way they function.

Some of them have formal contracts with one or more funeral homes that offer special discounts—as much as 50 percent off regular prices—in return for the volume of business assured by the society. Others have no formal contract but deal on an informal, cooperative basis with one or more local funeral homes, continuously monitoring their services and charges.

Even if neither the deceased nor the survivors have a current membership, a local memorial society may be willing to offer immediate membership or a referral to a funeral home with which it has dealings. Once in touch with a recommended funeral home, survivors can usually make whatever arrangements they prefer with reasonable confidence that they will be treated fairly.

FUNERAL HOMES

If their state does not license direct-disposal firms, if the community does not have a memorial society, or if the survivors prefer services that are not available from either, they will need to deal with a funeral home. Because this is the situation with which most survivors are faced, it is important for them to understand how to negotiate for what they want. It is here that you, as the executor, can play a vital role.

HOW FUNERALS ARE PRICED

The goods and services offered by the typical funeral home generally include the following:

Casket

Vault (unless a grave liner is purchased from the cemetery)

Professional services:
  embalming
  cosmetic restoration

Use of funeral home and facilities:
  for visitation and viewing
  for ritual service

Transportation:
  for body, from place of death to funeral home
  for body, from funeral home to disposal site (via house of
    worship if desired)

for mourners and pallbearers, to and from disposal site
for flowers, to disposal site (via house of worship if desired)
Other services:
  professional pallbearers
  visitors' register
  acknowledgment cards
  application for death benefits
Outlays on behalf of survivors:
  crematorium charges or cemetery costs—grave, and opening
    and closing charges
  copies of death certificate
  newspaper obituary notices
  flowers for casket
  clothing for body (if not provided by survivors)
  clergy fee
  fee for music provided

Some of these services are, of course, optional, and not all of them are included in what is called, in the language of the trade, a "standard adult funeral." They are listed here simply to provide the context for the several pricing methods used by funeral homes.

Many funeral homes currently use the *unit pricing system:* They quote a single price that includes the casket and some of the services listed above for a "standard adult funeral." Under this system, the price of the funeral depends on the price of the casket selected by the customer, but the services remain the same in number and quality regardless of the casket price. Outlays on behalf of the survivors—for cemetery plot, obituary notices, and so on—are not included.

Some funeral homes have adopted a *two-unit pricing system*, quoting one price for their professional services and another for the casket. Under this system, the various services provided are specified but are not priced individually.

A third system (advocated by the Federal Trade Commission but currently used by a minority of funeral homes) is called *item pricing*. As the term implies, each component of the funeral, whether essential or optional, is priced separately, and the price list is offered to the customer before any arrangements are made.

Item pricing would seem to be the best system from the survivors' point of view. It enables them to compare prices not only among funeral homes offering item pricing but also with those using the unit or two-unit pricing system. Armed with a list of item prices, they may be able to negotiate both services and prices with funeral homes offering the "standard adult funeral."

But item pricing is not widely used. Some funeral homes offer an itemized list but insert prices only after discussion with the customer. In such a situation, the survivors can't know whether the prices are standard, whether the funeral director has adjusted them to what he perceives to be their income level, or whether he has raised them to compensate for their choice of a low-priced casket. Moreover, if the survivors reject one of the items (embalming, for example), they may be forced to accept another item (refrigeration of the body).

If the survivors are not overwhelmed by grief or by time pressures, their most effective way to buy funeral services is to decide in advance—at least tentatively—which services they want and to try to get itemized or comparable quotations from two or more funeral homes. They may be able to do this without going from one home to another. Once they have the itemized list in hand, they may be able to get price information by telephone, even if their state law does not require funeral homes to provide it.

Most funeral homes are reluctant to quote prices by telephone because, they argue, misunderstandings are inevitable when customers do not know which services they want, which are essential, and which are included in the quoted price. Critics of the industry, on the other hand, maintain that this resistance to telephone price quotation stems from the funeral director's desire to "get hold of the body," or at least the customer, before discussing prices. But if the survivors can communicate to the funeral director that they know precisely what they want and that they plan to compare his quotations with those of his competitors, they may get results. If not, they may be able to enlist one or two friends or relatives, equip them with the list, and have them visit several funeral homes to compare prices on everything except the casket, since this is a choice that the survivors probably want to make personally.

To help the survivors prepare this list, we shall describe briefly the goods and services offered by the typical funeral home.

CASKET

The casket—usually the most expensive component of the funeral and the most profitable for the funeral director—can range in price from less than five hundred to several thousand dollars. A casket is generally bought—or, more accurately, sold—on the basis of three kinds of appeal. The first of these fosters the illusion that the corpse is somehow alive and is therefore sensitive to physical discomfort and to the attitudes of the survivors. This explains the sale of luxuriously upholstered caskets based on the suggestion that they are more comfortable. It also justifies the argument that "this is the last thing you can do for your father," the implication being that the deceased's feelings will be hurt if the survivors choose a casket that is something less than luxurious.

A second appeal capitalizes on the survivors' fantasies about decay of the corpse. Expensive one-piece or hermetically sealed caskets are often urged upon the survivors with the implication that they will postpone decay. Exhumations have provided fairly conclusive evidence, however, that the construction or sealing of the casket has little or no effect on the rate of decay—even if this were a desirable goal. Casket manufacturers who offer a 10- or 20-year guarantee that their product will remain intact are quite safe in doing so, because they are altogether unlikely to be presented with claims by unsatisfied buyers. Both the Federal Trade Commission Funeral Rule and some state regulations prohibit any claims that caskets postpone or prevent decay, and most funeral directors don't make them, but a good deal of casket salesmanship relies on this claim, which is usually subtly suggested rather than explicitly stated.

A third appeal implies that because it is the most conspicuous element in the funeral, the casket is an important indicator of social status—that a "quality" casket advertises the socioeconomic level of both the deceased and the survivors, as well as the survivors' love and respect for the deceased.

The choice of a casket may be influenced not only by the survivors' susceptibility to these appeals but also by their preferences for other elements of the funeral. If they plan to choose an open casket for viewing of the body, they may feel that the casket will be the focus of considerable attention. A closed casket, on the other hand, plays a less conspicuous part in any ritual, and an inexpensive model can be covered with a pall or with a spray of flowers. If the survivors choose cremation, they will need only an inexpensive container; and if cremation is to be preceded by a ritual service with the body present, it can, in some states, be placed in a rented casket; in other states the cremation container can be inserted into a rented casketlike enclosure.

Entering the casket display room to make a selection is, for many survivors, the most traumatic episode of the entire bereavement process, and their emotional state makes a rational selection difficult. Although the Federal Trade Commission Funeral Rule and many state laws require that a certain number of caskets in the lowest price range be displayed in every funeral home, some funeral directors place the least expensive model in inconspicuous, poorly lighted corners of the display room and, by subtle arrangement of lighting and furnishing, focus the customer's attention on the more expensive models. This wordless "bait and switch" tactic is sometimes reinforced by a display of the least attractive versions of the cheaper models (even though more attractive models are readily available), or by gestures, facial expressions, or even remarks of disapproval when the customer shows interest in the less expensive models.

If the survivors don't like any of the models on display, they should ask to see the manufacturers' catalogues; any model they list can usually be delivered promptly. If the style of the casket doesn't matter, they should inquire about the price of the Orthodox Jewish casket. Because religious law requires that this be a plain wooden box devoid of any ornamentation, it is likely to be inexpensive, and it is available almost everywhere. Many people like its simplicity and austerity.

VAULT OR GRAVE LINER

Once they have chosen a casket and decided on grave burial, the survivors are likely to be offered a vault—a container in which the casket is enclosed in the grave. Although they may be told that the vault serves to "protect" the casket (and hence, presumably, the body), its actual purpose is to prevent the ground level of the grave site from sinking as the earth settles or the casket decays with the passage of time. This purpose is served just as effectively by a cast-concrete grave liner, which can be bought from the cemetery at a substantially lower price.

Neither vaults nor grave liners are required by any state law, and funeral directors who imply that they are should be regarded with suspicion. Some states, however, allow individual cemeteries to require a liner as a condition of burial.

EMBALMING

Embalming involves the replacement of the blood and other bodily fluids with a preservative solution that retards decay. If it is to be effective in preserving the body for viewing in an open-casket ritual, it must be done within about eight hours of death. If the body is intended as an anatomic gift, however, embalming will render it unacceptable unless it is done under the supervision of the donee medical school, hospital, or organ bank.

No state requires embalming in all cases, and some states (as well as the Federal Trade Commission Funeral Rule) prohibit it without the consent of a survivor, but all states require it in certain circumstances, such as death from a communicable disease, delay in body disposal, or interstate transportation of the body.

Embalming is not necessary if the survivors choose direct disposal, and it is usually unnecessary if they choose cremation followed by a memorial service—although California, presumably under pressure from the funeral industry, requires embalming if the body is held more than 24 hours but prohibits cremation sooner than 48 hours after death.

COSMETIC RESTORATION

Cosmetic restoration is unnecessary if a closed casket or direct-disposal procedure is chosen, but when an open casket is used, most survivors insist on it. An unrestored corpse is gray (because blood has left the surface capillaries), with open mouth and staring eyes, but these inescapable facts of death are likely to be traumatic to the survivors and to other mourners, who would like to see the deceased "as we remember him."

On the other hand, the quality of the restoration is something of a gamble. Some funeral directors do a remarkable job of producing a likeness but, in the process, reduce the deceased's apparent age by 10 or 20 years. Others produce a gross caricature that severely distresses the survivors and cannot be corrected to their satisfaction once the body is ready for viewing.

CLOTHING

For open-casket viewing, the body will, of course, have to be clothed, and many funeral homes offer a wide array of styles and colors. There is no reason whatever to buy this merchandise if a favorite dress or suit belonging to the deceased is available.

VIEWING, VISITATION, AND RITUAL FACILITIES

If the survivors choose an open casket, they will probably want to use the funeral home for visitation and viewing, and they will recognize that there are charges for the use of these facilities. If they choose a closed casket, however, they may prefer to invite mourners to visit at home, in which case the casket can be stored at the funeral home until burial, and the funeral home charges reduced accordingly.

The same holds true for the use of the funeral home for any kind of ritual service. If the survivors plan a memorial service at home or elsewhere after the body has been disposed of, or if a service is to be held at a house of worship, there is no justification for the funeral home to charge for the use of its chapel, although there will be a charge for transporting the body to and from the house of worship.

One alternative, which represents a compromise between direct disposal and a traditional funeral, is a graveside service with a closed casket. Although the funeral home may impose a charge for additional time at the grave site, this should be more than offset by elimination of the charges for the use of the chapel, for viewing, and possibly for embalming and restoration. The graveside service is commonly used when death has occurred far from home and the casket is brought directly from the airport to the cemetery.

TRANSPORTATION CHARGES

The "standard adult funeral" usually includes charges for transporting the body from the place of death to the funeral home and thence to the cemetery or crematorium, and for one limousine to transport the principal mourners to and from the disposal site. The need for additional limousines will be based, of course, on the number and the emotional states of the mourners, but usually such a decision can be made at the last minute—during the ritual service, if necessary. Generally most mourners can be relied on to drive their own cars and to provide space in them for those who don't.

OTHER SERVICES

The typical funeral home provides a number of miscellaneous services that should be specified at the time that the initial arrangements are made, whether or not their cost is itemized.

Death Certificates

In settling the estate, you will need a certified copy of the death certificate in order to transfer ownership of *each* piece of real estate, *each* stock certificate, and *each* motor vehicle; to collect the benefits payable under *each* insurance policy; to collect *each* death benefit; and for a variety of other purposes, such as gaining entry to the deceased's safe deposit box.

Virtually all funeral homes will offer to obtain these certificates for you from the local county clerk or the health department, but there are two problems connected with this offer. First, although some funeral homes provide this service at cost—the nominal fee charged by the issuing office—others add a surcharge, which you can avoid by getting the copies yourself. Second, because it is virtually impossible for you to know precisely how many copies you will need, you are likely to order either too many or too few. The best plan may be to order only the minimum number you need immediately and to obtain additional copies as the need arises.

Death Benefits

Funeral homes may offer to file applications on the survivors' behalf for any Social Security or Veterans Administration burial benefits to which they are entitled, but often they will do this only if the benefits are to be applied to the funeral bill. Although this service may relieve the estate of responsibility for part of the funeral bill, and although it eliminates your having to file the applications yourself and wait for payment, it has one disadvantage. If the final bill is presented with the burial benefits already credited, you may regard the bill as reasonable, whereas the total bill may, in fact, be unreasonably high and hence challengeable. If, on the other hand, you pay the entire bill with estate funds, you will reduce the estate's net assets and thus possibly reduce estate or inheritance taxes.

Crematorium or Cemetery Arrangements

If the deceased did not own a cemetery plot and if arrangements have not been made for disposal of the body, the funeral director can help choose a cemetery or a crematorium and will add the charges to his bill. In some circumstances, this service can be very helpful, because funeral directors are usually well acquainted with the community's cemeteries and crematoriums. As we shall see shortly, however, problems can arise when the funeral home advances substantial sums of money on behalf of the estate.

Obituary Notices

Many funeral directors will offer to place paid obituary notices in the appropriate local and national newspapers and to help with the wording of the notice. Their experience can be useful, because many grief-stricken survivors tend either to omit essential information from the notice or to overload it with unnecessary detail.

CASH OUTLAYS BY THE FUNERAL HOME

A number of the services described above—for example, obtaining death certificates, placing obituary notices, buying a grave plot—involve cash disbursements by the funeral director. In addition, the funeral director may also add to the bill gratuities for the hearse and limousine drivers and for the gravediggers.

At first glance, it would appear that the funeral director's willingness to take care of all these transactions spares the survivors a good deal of effort and inconvenience when they are under stress—as is often the case. But critics of the funeral industry point out that this convenience is not always free of charge. Some funeral directors bill customers for an amount greater than the sum of their disbursements; others receive discounts (for obituary notices, for example) that they fail to pass on to the customer. Worse yet, in some instances clergymen, organists, and soloists complain that they never receive the honorarium for which the funeral home has billed and collected from the customer.

There is something to be said, therefore, for handling some of these disbursements personally. Since survivors are unlikely to select a grave site or a crematorium sight unseen, they may as well make the arrangements when they inspect the site. They may want to see to it, also, that their honorarium for the clergyman reaches its intended recipient, especially since a check made payable to the house of worship rather than to the individual is tax deductible as a charitable contribution.

SPECIFYING THE FINAL DETAILS

The funeral director is in the ethically difficult position of having to *advise* the customer about which goods and services to choose and, at the same time, to *sell* them to the customer. This is why survivors who don't know exactly what they want and put themselves into the hands of a funeral director whose entrepreneurial role requires him to maximize profit are rather likely to be exploited. After reading this chapter, however, you should have a reasonably clear idea of what you want and, more important, what you don't need or don't want. And just as you have learned to disregard or reject the opportuning of the automobile salesman who tries to sell you expensive options, so, too, you should feel quite comfortable about rejecting funeral goods and services that strike you as inappropriate or unnecessary.

Despite the absence of prices in its advertising, the funeral industry is highly competitive. Every funeral director knows that an inexpensive funeral service is better than no service at all, and some may feel forced to forego any profit merely to pay their continuing overhead costs. Consequently, if survivors come to the funeral home with a clearly defined set of specifications and convey the impression that they are there to *buy* a funeral and not to be *sold* one, they are likely to get exactly what they want, and at a competitive price.

DEALING WITH A CREMATORIUM

Unlike the funeral home industry, the crematorium industry is not overcrowded and, except in metropolitan areas, choice among competing firms is likely to be limited. And, again unlike funeral homes, crematoriums do not offer an essentially identical range of services. Some firms, catering mainly to survivors who choose direct disposal, provide only a crematory service, which includes delivery of the ashes to the survivor in a sealed canister. Others provide, in addition, viewing and visitation facilities and a chapel for a ritual service. Still others provide facilities for scattering the ashes in a garden or for storing them permanently in a niche in a columbarium. This wide range of services makes price comparison difficult.

In general, however, the guiding principle should probably be simplicity. The choice of cremation rather than burial is made more often by the deceased than by the survivors, and if the survivors disagree with it, they can disregard it. Hence, those survivors who comply with the deceased's wishes presumably share the philosophy underlying the decision: a lack of emphasis on the physical remains. With this in mind, they are less likely to seek preservation of the ashes in a decorative urn set permanently in a columbarium niche, and more likely to see cremation as a method of swiftly returning the body to its basic elements.

SEEKING REDRESS

Because funeral negotiations usually take place under severe emotional stress and time pressure, survivors may, despite their best efforts, be misled, overcharged, or cheated. Since you, as the executor, are likely to be responsible for settling the final funeral bill, you should scrutinize it carefully and question any doubtful items before paying it.

Your first step (and the easiest one) is to discuss any questionable or disputed issues with the funeral director, in the hope that the difficulty stemmed from an error or a misunderstanding rather than from any fraudulent intent. If this meeting does not resolve the problem, there are several organizations with which you can lodge a complaint.

Your state's "mortuary board"—the administrative body that controls the licensing of funeral directors—will entertain complaints against them, but the degree of cooperation and support you will receive depends on the state in which you live. Some boards include not only funeral directors but also "public members," whose explicit function is to represent and protect the interests of consumers; other boards consist entirely of funeral directors whose principal interest seems to be restricting entry into the profession and thus protecting current practitioners against newcomers and other competitors.

Another possible resource, the National Funeral Directors Association (13625 Bishops Dr. Brookfield, WI 53005 (800) 228-6332), sponsors an independent organization known as ThanaCAP, which arbitrates consumer disputes with funeral directors, whether or not they are members of the association.

Most state attorneys general administer a consumer protection division that processes and investigates consumer complaints and that can initiate civil or criminal action against chronic offenders.

The Federal Trade Commission will not investigate or resolve individual complaints, but will take action against chronically offending firms or against unethical practices that are widespread. It is the FTC that was responsible for drafting and enforcing the Funeral Rule, which has been highly effective in stopping certain deceptive practices throughout the industry.

As we have noted, if the deceased's estate is being, or will be, probated (see Chapter 7), you can consider withholding payment of a funeral bill that you regard as excessive or fraudulent. Under these conditions, the funeral home will have to file a creditor's claim in the probate proceedings, and you will have the opportunity to file your objections with the court, which may disallow all or part of the bill.

But before you take any action, you need to be as certain as possible that you are not directing against a perfectly honorable funeral director the understandable anger or resentment that you or the survivors feel over the death itself.

~ 5 ~

SORTING THE ASSETS
AND LIABILITIES

Your first step in settling the estate is to locate all the deceased's assets, identify those that were owned solely by the deceased, and preserve them until they can be sold or distributed according to the terms of the will or, if there was no will, according to the state intestacy laws. Similarly, you need to identify all the deceased's liabilities so that you can pay all his taxes and legitimate debts.

This task is relatively easy if the deceased left an up-to-date letter of instruction (see p. 25), which identifies each asset and liability and describes its location. But even if you have such a letter, you must look carefully for assets that may have been overlooked or that may have been acquired after the most recent draft.

On the other hand, if you find no letter of instruction and if you have not been intimately and currently in touch with the deceased's every financial transaction, you will need to undertake the following search in order to identify and assemble all the assets and liabilities.

SEARCHING FOR THE ASSETS

CHECKING ACCOUNTS

Your most useful "map" of the deceased's financial situation is likely to be his checkbook, bank statements, and file of canceled checks. A careful review of every check written and every deposit recorded during the year preceding the death should provide you with reliable information on the following:

Insurance policies—checks for premium payments will identify the insurance company and possibly each current life, accident, automobile, homeowners, and health insurance policy.

Mortgages and land contracts—payment checks can help you identify the properties subject to these liens.

Investments—checks can identify certificates of deposit, brokerage accounts, money market or mutual funds, recent specific purchases, and IRA, Keogh, SEP, or 401K accounts.

Charge accounts and loans—checks should help you identify creditors and determine the current level of indebtedness.

Taxes—checks will indicate the most recent payments and, hence, the amounts still payable. Property tax payments will identify owned properties.

Utility payments—bill payments can identify properties not revealed by tax or mortgage payments.

Hospital and medical expenses—payments should be checked against recent health care bills and against health care insurance for possible reimbursement.

Payments for goods and services not actually used—airline tickets that may be fully refundable, or magazine subscriptions that may be refundable pro rata.

License fees for cars and other vehicles—checks can identify vehicles owned by the deceased.

Charitable contributions—if you will be responsible for filing the deceased's individual income tax return.

Safe deposit box or post office box rental—so that you can locate these boxes and inventory their contents.

Your review of the checkbook may help you identify such sources of assets or future income as:

- Rents on income property
- Stock dividend and bond interest payments
- Payments on mortgages, land contracts, or promissory notes held by the deceased
- Royalties on patents, mineral rights, or books
- Insurance dividends—a clue to paid-up policies
- Tax refunds
- Social Security, Veterans Administration, and pension benefits
- Fees for consultation or other services
- Deposits for electric and telephone service

This review may not unearth every single asset. Some of the deceased's dividends may have been paid directly into a money market account, and some payments may have been made by money market fund checks. In addition, paid-up insurance policies that pay no dividends will not appear in the bank records. Nevertheless, tedious though it may be, your examination of the deceased's bank records will save you a great deal of time and trouble in settling the estate—especially since you may be responsible for filing the deceased's final income tax returns.

THE DECEASED'S MAIL

A second source of information about assets and liabilities is the mail that will continue to arrive for the deceased because, in addition to advertising and social correspondence, it is likely to contain dividend and pension checks, bank and brokerage statements, payments on debts owed to the deceased, utility and tax bills, and bills or notices about insurance premiums, charge accounts, and other liabilities.

The postal regulations governing delivery of the deceased's mail are reasonably clear. When the local post office learns of the death of a mail recipient (either through formal notification or, informally, through the mail carrier, who may notice mail accumulating at the address), it will hold the mail for 15 days and then return it to the sender.

Most of the deceased's mail can be claimed at the post office or readdressed by means of the usual change-of-address form, either by a family member or another survivor who can provide the postmaster with satisfactory identification and a copy of the death certificate. As the executor, you can use the same method once you can provide the postmaster with a copy of your letters of authority (see p. 131).

But not all of the deceased's mail will be available to you through this procedure. Most U.S. Treasury checks—for Social Security or Veterans Administration benefits, for example, but not income tax refunds—must be returned by the postmaster to the sending agency. Other government checks—state, county, or municipal—must be handled in accordance with instructions printed on their envelopes, as must mail containing driver's licenses, vehicle registrations, credit cards, and other documents intended for the exclusive use of the deceased.

If the deceased rented a post office box, you can continue to collect all mail, but you are obligated to return to the sender the U.S. Treasury checks and other mail mentioned in the preceding paragraph. Usually, however, executors prefer to use a change-of-address form rather than making regular trips to a post office box.

Normally the mail collection procedure works smoothly, but occasionally problems arise: the postmaster may, for example, receive two different change-of-address forms, each signed by a different person, either because these survivors are in conflict or because they failed to communicate with one another. In such a situation you, as executor, have final authority, because the postmaster is required by law to honor your letters of authority and comply with your instructions.

As you receive the deceased's mail, your first step is to sort out any mail addressed to joint owners (bank statements, dividend checks, bills, and so on) and give or send it to the surviving owner, because none of it constitutes part of the deceased's assets or liabilities. The rest of the mail should be sorted into five categories:

- Assets—dividend checks and other items payable to the deceased alone
- Liabilities—credit card and charge account statements, utility bills, premium notices, tax bills, and other notices of payments due
- Social correspondence
- Magazine subscriptions
- Advertising and other "junk" mail

The handling of assets and liabilities will be dealt with later in this chapter and in Chapter 6. Social correspondence can be answered by you or by a family member or by means of a simple printed announcement of the death. Magazine subscriptions, if they are of no interest to the survivors, can be transferred to a friend or a local library or, if relatively recent, can be canceled with a request for a refund for all future issues. Advertising mail can, of course, be discarded when received.

Although the volume of mail is likely to diminish rapidly, you should continue to monitor it conscientiously for at least six months and preferably for a year. Some banks, money market funds, IRA, Keogh, and 401K account managers, and other investment facilities issue statements or pay capital gains only annually; most bond interest is payable semiannually; and many certificates of deposit have terms of one year or more. In addition, some insurance premiums are payable semiannually or annually. Hence, unless you monitor the mail over an extended period of time, you may over-look both assets and liabilities.

There is no need, however, to delay settling the estate in the hope that such assets may turn up later. It is always possible to reopen the probate estate after closure for the purpose of settling and distributing newly discovered assets.

THE SAFE DEPOSIT BOX

Like the deceased's mail, the safe deposit box may contain actual assets (cash, collectibles, or jewelry) or documentary evidence of assets (such as insurance policies, property deeds and land contracts, stock certificates, bills of sale, receipts, vehicle titles and registrations, savings passbooks, money market certificates, promissory notes, mortgages, and the like). In addition, the box may contain a will, a letter of instruction, a property inventory, or other documents identifying the location and ownership of certain assets. It may also contain a record of military service.

Unless you are a surviving joint lessee of the box, you may not be aware of its existence, but it is a mistake to assume that one does not exist. If your review of the bank record fails to disclose a payment for box rental, look among the deceased's personal belongings for a flat, multi-notched key usually stored in a small envelope bearing the bank's name, or inquire at all the banks at which the deceased maintained an account or conducted business.

Access to the box and its contents may present difficulties. Even though you are an executor armed with letters of authority (see p. 131), banks in some states, on learning of the lessee's death, "seal" the box until it can be opened in the presence of a representative of the state treasury department, who will inventory the contents for tax purposes.

In those states that require it, requesting a state treasury representative to make the inventory is quite simple, and any bank officer will do it (or tell you how to do it) without delay. Although its primary purpose is to protect the state against tax evasion, it can also protect you in case of a dispute among the interested parties (beneficiaries, heirs at law, and creditors) as to what was or was not in the box when it was opened. In any event, you should not open the box unaccompanied, because this leaves you vulnerable to all sorts of accusations with respect to its contents. If several beneficiaries are available, have them accompany you and sign or initial a dated inventory of the contents.

The fact that a box was leased jointly (usually with a spouse) does not in itself constitute conclusive evidence that its contents are jointly owned. In fact, unless there is good evidence to the contrary, the contents of the box may be presumed to be the sole property of the deceased and hence to require probate as part of the deceased's estate. Stock certificates and bonds registered in joint ownership are, of course, the property of the surviving owner, but untitled assets (such as cash) and such items as coin collections, precious stones or metals, and other valuables may be considered to be the sole property of the deceased unless there is documentary evidence to prove joint ownership. Women's jewelry found in a jointly leased box will be presumed to belong to the woman, but the ownership of such jewelry found in a box leased jointly by two brothers will depend on such documentary evidence as receipts, bills of sale, canceled checks, or written statements of ownership.

Once the contents of the box have been inventoried, any jointly owned assets should be delivered to the surviving joint owner. Those that are owned solely by the deceased must be protected against theft, loss, or damage until they are sold or distributed to the beneficiaries by one of the processes described in Chapters 6 and 7. One way to do this is to store them in a safe deposit box leased in your own name so that you will have access to them at any time.

ACCESSING
SOLELY OWNED ASSETS

Your search is likely to turn up several kinds of assets that require no further action on your part. Any assets—securities, bank accounts, real estate, for example—that the deceased held jointly with someone else pass automatically to the surviving joint owner unless the joint owner died before or simultaneously with the deceased. Similarly, any assets held in a living trust remain under the control of the trustee or successor trustee, who must hold or distribute them according to the terms of the trust document (see

Chapter 11). Bank and brokerage accounts, securities certificates, and mutual funds subject to pay-on-death or transfer-on-death provisions pass to the designated beneficiary. Unless a designated beneficiary is the estate itself, life insurance proceeds will be paid to the named beneficiaries as soon as the insurance company receives a claim accompanied by proof of the death of the insured. As for any Social Security or Veterans Administration burial allowance, this is usually applied for by the funeral director, who will deduct it from the funeral bill.

But some assets—a savings or checking account, for example, wages or salary not yet paid to the deceased, a motor vehicle, or a boat—may have belonged solely to the deceased. As we shall see in Chapter 6, some of these assets can be transferred informally to a surviving spouse or next of kin, and others. If they do not exceed the state-imposed maximum values, they can be transferred by an affidavit procedure or by a simplified form of probate. If, however, a substantial amount of probate assets is involved, full probate administration is required, as explained in Chapter 7.

MANAGING THE LIQUID ASSETS

The best way to consolidate the deceased's liquid probate assets, to pay the deceased's taxes and debts, and to pay and keep track of your administrative expenses as the executor is to open a bank checking account under the title "John Jones, Executor of the Estate of Mary Smith, Deceased." Into this account you can deposit all of the deceased's cash on hand, solely owned bank balances, dividends, proceeds from the sale of estate assets, certificates of deposit as they mature, payments on debts owed to the deceased, and any other moneys belonging to the estate that you receive between the time of death and completing the administration of the probate estate. From this estate account you can write checks to pay the deceased's taxes and lawful debts, to pay bond premiums, to compensate others employed by you as executor, to reimburse your expenses and pay your fees (if any), to pay court costs, and to make final distribution of the balance to the entitled beneficiaries.

The type of bank account you choose needs careful consideration. On the one hand, a checking account is necessary if it is to be used to pay the deceased's taxes, creditors, and any other legitimate expenses you incur. On the other hand, if you are to protect these moneys from the effects of inflation and attempt to maximize their yield until the estate is settled, some kind of interest-bearing account would be advisable.

In general, any type of account that is federally insured (by the FDIC or the SLIC) may be used. Such accounts usually yield a lower interest rate than some uninsured short-term investments, such as money market funds, but no uninsured investment should be made without the express consent of all the beneficiaries and creditors or of the probate court or the clear authorization by state law.

DEALING WITH NONLIQUID ASSETS

Assets that are liquid or the proceeds of those that can be liquidated immediately can be deposited promptly into your executor's bank account. But several types of assets cannot reasonably be liquidated immediately, and these need careful consideration.

HOUSE AND CONTENTS

In many, if not most, cases, the home and its contents constitute the most valuable part of the deceased's assets and hence are of critical importance to the survivors. If the home was owned jointly (often with a surviving spouse), its ownership passes automatically to the surviving owner without any need for probate administration. The surviving joint owner need only record a certified copy of the deceased's death certificate with the register of deeds in the county in which the home is located. This establishes as a matter of public record that the surviving joint owner is now the sole owner and is therefore exclusively entitled to possess, occupy, rent, mortgage, sell, or otherwise control the property. The same applies to any other jointly held real estate—a vacation home or commercial income property.

If the home is titled in the name of the trustee of a living trust (see p. 44), the settlement procedure is slightly more involved. Depending on the terms of the trust, the trustee or successor trustee will either hold the home or other real estate in the trust, sell it, or deed it to the beneficiary designated in the trust document and then record the new deed with the register of deeds. As is the case with jointly held property, no probate court administration is required.

If, however, the home (or other real estate) was titled solely in the name of the deceased, probate administration will be required. Meanwhile, you, as the executor, must protect the property and its contents against loss or damage until the estate is fully settled. This means that you must make regular mortgage payments if failure to make them will result in default, penalty, or foreclosure. Similarly, you must pay utility and heating bills if termination of service poses a threat to the home or its contents. And, for the same reason, insurance coverage for fire, burglary, and liability must be maintained by prompt payment of premiums. All of these expenses are payable from estate funds. If you must pay them out of your own pocket, you are entitled to reimbursement from estate funds.

As executor, you may have the responsibility for selling the home and for paying any associated costs—for appraisal, for example, or for closing the sale—out of the proceeds of the sale or from your executor's bank account.

The fact that a home was owned jointly by the deceased does not mean, strictly speaking, that its contents were also owned jointly. In practice, however, joint ownership is assumed, and the contents pass to the surviving joint owner except for items specifically determined to be solely owned and willed to other people—a stamp collection, for example, or a piece of antique furniture. Such items can be willed, however, only if they can be proved (by means of a receipt or bill of sale, for example) to have been solely owned by the deceased. If, for example, the deceased's will bequeaths a valuable shotgun to a friend, the surviving spouse may contest the bequest on grounds that it was purchased with money earned by both spouses, with a credit card issued to both of them, or that the deceased left written evidence specifying that the shotgun was owned jointly with the spouse. If an item is proven to be solely owned by the deceased, it is a probate asset and passes according to the will and, if there was no will, according to state intestacy laws. If it is proven to have been a lifetime gift, the recipient keeps it even if the will bequeaths it to someone else.

ACCOUNTS RECEIVABLE

If the estate's assets include payments that are due the deceased over a considerable length of time—for royalties on books, patents, or mineral rights, for example, or promissory notes or land contracts held by the deceased—final distribution of the probate estate usually includes the transfer of these contract rights to the beneficiaries designated in the will. If this is not done, the probate estate cannot be closed until the last payment is received—sometimes a period of several years.

The deceased's solely owned "accounts receivable" payments are probate assets, but payroll checks and employee benefits may not be if arrangements can be made to have them paid directly to the beneficiaries (see Chapter 6). Hence, they should not be deposited in your executor's account until this determination has been made.

MOTOR VEHICLES

Motor vehicles may have been owned solely by the deceased, jointly with a survivor, or in the name of the trustee of a living trust. In most states, however, ownership of solely owned vehicles can be transferred immediately to specified survivors without requiring probate administration. The state department of motor vehicles, when presented with a copy of the deceased's death certificate, simply transfers the titles of vehicles to certain next of kin or to the person designated by state law.

SECURITIES

Securities held in the name of the deceased alone should not be liquidated until you have determined whether they may be transferable directly to the beneficiaries through one of the "small estate" transfer procedures described in Chapter 6. If this is clearly impracticable, they can be sold immediately or held for later distribution to the beneficiaries. You may feel that stock prices are low at the moment and that holding them until market conditions improve will result in a higher yield. But since nobody can predict the course of the stock market, you should consider selling them immediately unless you have the consent of all the beneficiaries to delay selling.

"WRONGFUL-DEATH" CLAIMS

A possible source of assets that you may easily overlook is money damages that may be recoverable if the deceased's death was caused, in whole or in part, by the intentional or negligent behavior of someone else. Although such damage claims are probably most common when death is due to an automobile accident, it is also possible to sue physicians, hospitals, and other health care providers for failure to make a correct diagnosis or provide appropriate medical care. Similarly, suit may be brought against building owners for structural defects or inadequate maintenance, against manufacturers and retailers of unsafe or defective products, against employers for failure to provide a safe work environment, and against police departments for use of excessive force that resulted in death.

Some commentators, citing the rise in medical malpractice claims, conclude that we are becoming an increasingly litigious society. But the proliferation of such claims can also be explained by the fact that more people are receiving medical care and are better informed about their legal rights and remedies. Others argue that many legitimate wrongful-death claims are never pursued simply because the survivors fail to recognize that they have a viable claim or because they feel that filing a lawsuit is probably not worth the time, effort, psychological stress, and possible costs.

If the deceased's death can be linked in any way to someone's intentional or negligent act or omission, you should make every effort to identify the person or persons involved and discuss promptly with a skilled personal injury lawyer the possibility of pursuing a claim for money damages.

In considering such a claim, you need to bear in mind two well-established legal principles. First, the death need not have occurred immediately after the negligent act; the recovery of money damages may be justified even if the death occurred many months after the precipitating event. Second, under the laws of many states, it is not necessary that the wrongdoer's negligence be 100 percent responsible for the death. Even if the wrongdoer's behavior is found by the judge or jury to be only 25 percent responsible, the other 75 percent having been caused by the deceased's contributory negligence, 25 percent of the claimed damages may be recoverable by the deceased's estate or the survivors.

Examples of successful negligence suits are not hard to find, and those presented here should help you understand that the underlying negligence need not always be clearly apparent or immediately present. In cases of death by fire, building owners have been successfully sued for maintaining unsafe premises or violating fire codes even though the victim had been smoking in bed. Owners of swimming pools have been held responsible for leaving open a gate through which a child wandered and subsequently drowned, even though the parents may have been negligent in the supervision of the child. And, of course, automobile manufacturers have been sued as a result of deaths attributed to faulty vehicle design or manufacture, even though the driver's behavior may have precipitated the accident in whole or in part. It is a mistake, therefore, to assume that a wrongful-death claim will necessarily be unsuccessful simply because the deceased's arguably negligent behavior contributed in part to the injury and resulting death.

Two further considerations may discourage you from pursuing a wrongful-death claim. First, there is the notion that the negligent party is not worth suing "because he obviously hasn't enough money to pay a judgment of any size." This conclusion is premature until the possibility of liability insurance coverage has been fully explored—especially in states with compulsory automobile liability insurance. Second, many people believe that a lawsuit is too expensive to file, even if the prospect of eventual recovery seems favorable. Actually, the cost of pursuing a wrongful-death claim need not be a deterrent, because most lawyers who take such cases are willing to do so on a "contingent fee" basis: If the lawyer recovers money damages, he or she is entitled to keep a specified portion (usually one-third of the net recovery) as a fee for legal services. If the lawyer loses and recovers nothing, he or she receives no fee at all.

Although the contingent-fee arrangement has been called "the poor man's key to the courthouse," and although it would appear to make wrongful-death claims affordable by anyone, it is not without its problems. The processing of a claim typically requires the lawyer to incur out-of-pocket expenses—for purchasing transcripts and other records, for hiring expert witnesses, for taking depositions and conducting investigations, and for the payment of court costs. These expenses, though advanced by the lawyer, are ultimately chargeable to the client, whether the case is won or lost. Thus, if the estate fails to win the suit, it may face legal costs of several thousand dollars. If you, as executor, approach a lawyer about filing suit, therefore, be sure to discuss not only the contingent fee but also the anticipated amount of out-of-pocket expenses.

Although many survivors fail to initiate a wrongful-death claim even when there is a valid basis for such an action, there are others who are all too eager to bring suit. This occurs not necessarily because they are naturally litigious but because they are trying to find an outlet for the frustration and grief caused by the death. If a close relative dies after surgery, for example, the survivors may allege faulty work by the surgeon or improper care by the hospital staff even though both surgeon and staff may have performed in exemplary fashion.

One might think that a lawyer's negative opinion about the merits of the case would deter such people from bringing suit, since few lawyers are likely to reject the pursuit of a claim that has merit. But because the motivations for bringing such suits are largely psychological, any objective opinion from the lawyer to the effect that the claim is without merit may lead only to a search for a lawyer with a different opinion.

If you believe that you have grounds for a claim, you should consult a lawyer immediately, because often such claims must be filed within two to three years following the death and because critical evidence—for example, autopsy results, medical records, photographs of an accident scene, preservation of a wrecked automobile or its parts—must be gathered and preserved while it is still fresh. Finding a competent personal-injury lawyer may be as difficult as finding one experienced in estate planning, because this is a field crowded with lawyers seeking such often lucrative cases. The state bar association's lawyer referral service is a far more reliable source than the Yellow Pages or television and Internet commercials.

Once you and the lawyer sign a contingent-fee agreement, he or she will investigate the merits of the claim and the financial condition or the insurance coverage of the wrongdoer. The lawyer will then submit a claim to the wrongdoer or the insurer setting forth the claim's factual and legal basis and demanding monetary compensation for some or all of the following items of damage:

- Conscious pain and suffering experienced by the deceased before death
- Ambulance, hospital, and medical expenses
- Funeral and burial expenses
- Loss of income or support that the deceased would have provided for his dependents had he enjoyed his full life expectancy
- Loss of the society and companionship that the deceased would have provided to his family

If the decedent's claim has merit and if the wrongdoer has sufficient assets or insurance coverage, the response to your lawyer is likely to be an offer of an out-of-court settlement, for an amounts somewhat less than you initially demanded. Your lawyer may or may not be able to negotiate an increase in the settlement offer, but acceptance of it will provide the beneficiaries with immediate cash, avoid the delay, expense, and uncertainty of a trial, and eliminate your anxiety about a procedure with which you and other survivors are likely to be unfamiliar.

Although estates involving wrongful-death claims generally must be probated, you can explore the possibility of pursuing such a claim before you have been appointed as executor, especially since personal-injury lawyers are usually willing to provide an initial consultation at no cost. But a suit should not be initiated until you have been formally appointed; otherwise the litigation costs may be charged to you personally rather than to the estate and the court may rule that you lack standing to file suit in your individual capacity.

In some states, moneys recovered through a wrongful-death claim become probate assets and are distributed to the will-designated beneficiaries or heirs. In other states, however, payment of the recovery must be made directly to certain survivors specified by applicable wrongful-death laws.

PROTECTING THE ASSETS

Until they are distributed to the beneficiaries, you, as the executor, are responsible for safeguarding the probate assets and protecting them against loss or depreciation. Bear in mind in this connection (1) that your letters of authority (see Chapter 7) give you both the right and the responsibility to manage the estate according to the terms of the will, and (2) that you are entitled to charge against the estate any costs and fees you incur in connection with managing it.

DEALING WITH
THE LIABILITIES

As you continue to review the deceased's mail, you will almost certainly find bills, statements, premium notices, and other evidence of debts. Bills for goods and services that have been bought jointly, or through a joint charge account or credit card, remain the responsibility of the estate as well as the surviving joint debtor. If the estate has sufficient assets, the surviving debtor may prefer that the estate take care of the debt in due course. But if the estate's assets are insufficient and the surviving debtor wants to preserve a satisfactory credit rating and avoid interest charges, the debt should be paid promptly.

Bills incurred by the deceased alone, however, may confront you with a dilemma. Strictly speaking, these bills are payable by the estate, and hence you should not pay them until (1) you have been formally appointed as the executor, (2) you have determined that they are legitimate, and (3) you know that the estate has enough money to pay them. If the estate does not have enough money, these debts need not be paid. Furthermore, the "small estate" procedures in some states (see Chapter 6) permit the transfer of the deceased's probate assets to designated survivors without regard to the claims of creditors. All these considerations should lead you to postpone paying any such bills until you have a clear idea of the value of the probate assets and the type of probate procedure, if any, they will require.

On the other hand, failure to pay certain kinds of bills—mortgage payments, utility bills, taxes, charge accounts—may, as we have noted, harm the estate in one way or another. In such situations, whether or not you have been appointed as executor, you must use your best judgment. If you are convinced that the charges are legitimate and that the bills should be paid promptly, you can pay them out of your own pocket and be fully reimbursed from estate funds.

But doing this entails two risks. First, the estate may have insufficient assets to reimburse you, or the estate may have such low value that it is not required to pay any of its creditors (see Chapter 8). Second, the creditors of an estate are ranked by state law in a specific order of priority (see p. 148). Hence, if you pay a low-priority creditor, you may be held personally responsible for a high-priority creditor's unpaid claim. For these reasons you should probably postpone the payment of any bill that is reasonably postponable—at least until you have read Chapters 7 and 8.

Whether or not you decide to pay charge accounts promptly, the charge card should be destroyed or, in the case of credit cards, returned to the issuer. Destruction of a credit card will, of course, prevent its further use, but it will not terminate the annual fee. Returning the card to the bank or giving the bank prompt notice may produce a refund of part of the unused annual fee.

Because many survivors apparently feel that they are paying their respects to the deceased by settling all his outstanding debts regardless of their nature, it is important to recognize that in many cases they are under no legal obligation to do so. The Uniform Probate Code (see p. 111) provides that under certain circumstances the deceased's debts may be ignored. The intention here was to discourage survivors from depleting small estates because they felt obligated to prevent the deceased from "having died a debtor." Every creditor makes provision for a certain percentage of "bad debts," and there is no reason why survivors should not recognize this reality.

NEXT STEPS

Once you have sorted out the deceased's solely owned assets and liabilities, you will be in a position to determine your next steps.

If the deceased engaged in some careful estate planning, there is the possibility that all the assets will have been either jointly owned with someone who survived him, owned by the trustee of his living trust, or be payable on death to account-designated beneficiaries. In any of such cases, there will be no assets whatever to be collected by the executor and hence no need for probate administration. In such event, the probate court will be involved only if a guardian or conservator must be appointed to protect the deceased's minor or incompetent children.

A more likely situation is that there will be a few items, such as a checking or savings account balance, titled in the name of the deceased alone. In such circumstances, the estate may be eligible for what are known as "small estate" transfer procedures—swift, simple, and inexpensive asset-transfer provisions currently available in almost all states. These are discussed in Chapter 6.

If, however, the deceased's probate assets exceed the maximum values allowed under "small estate" transfer procedures, full probate-court administration may be required. This process will be dealt with in Chapter 7.

Part III

PROBATE ADMINISTRATION

~ 6 ~

AVOIDING OR
MINIMIZING PROBATE

Once you have assembled and evaluated all the deceased's assets, as described in Chapter 5, you are ready to proceed with settling and closing the estate. Your separation of the assets into probate and nonprobate categories should give you a fairly clear notion as to what, if any, probate procedures are necessary, because the value of the probate assets is a major factor in determining whether the estate must undergo full administration by the probate court or can be settled less formally.

Actually, the vast majority of estates are settled and closed without any intervention by the probate court. If the estate that you are involved with is typical, a reading of the next few pages should relieve you of any anxieties you may have concerning the estate settlement process.

WHEN IS PROBATE NECESSARY?

The basic purposes of probate are to protect minor children and their property, to see that the deceased's taxes and debts are paid, to determine the existence of a valid will, and to distribute the deceased's probate assets to the beneficiaries named in the will or, if the deceased left no will, to the heirs specified by state intestacy laws.

Obviously, if the deceased left no orphaned minor or incompetent children and no probate assets—because he owned nothing, or because everything he owned was given away before death, or was owned jointly, or was held in a trust, or consisted of life insurance or some other account or contract right that specified a designated beneficiary—there are no probate assets and hence nothing to probate. If this is the situation confronting you, there is no need for you to read the rest of this chapter.

Although some states permit creditors to file claims against a trust or its assets, creditors' claims against the deceased can sometimes be ignored when there are no probate assets. Nevertheless, it would be courteous (but not legally required) to inform creditors that the deceased left no assets with which to pay their bills. Of course, if the deceased's credit agreements were cosigned by someone—as is often the case in connection with credit cards, car loans, and home mortgages—the surviving cosigner remains responsible for these account balances. This same principle applies whether or not the deceased left a will. State laws requiring probate administration are based on the kind and value of property left by the deceased—not on the existence of a will.

Even if the deceased left probate assets, however, the estate can, in many cases, be settled by procedures that are simpler, quicker, and cheaper than full administration by the probate court. Some probate action may be necessary, however, in each of the following circumstances.

If the deceased left minor orphans—a not uncommon situation when husband and wife die simultaneously in an accident—the probate court must be involved in the appointment of a guardian for children and, if their inheritance is substantial, a conservator to manage each minor child's inheritance until the child reaches adulthood. This type of probate action is dealt with in Chapter 1, and it may not necessarily involve the court in administration of the deceased's estate. The estate itself, depending on its nature and value, may be eligible for one of the informal small-estate transfer procedures described below.

If the deceased died in circumstances giving rise to a wrongful-death claim (see p. 94), you, as the executor, should investigate and initiate a claim and possibly a lawsuit, sign settlement and release papers if money damages are recovered, and distribute the proceeds to survivors specified by state law.

If the deceased was covered by life insurance but (1) was not survived by a beneficiary designated in the policy or (2) designated his estate or executor as the beneficiary, the distribution of the insurance proceeds may require some action by the probate court, the precise procedure depending on the amount involved.

If the deceased left probate assets, you, as the nominated executor, must collect, protect, and manage them. But this in itself does not mean that full probate administration will be required. For example, household furnishings and appliances, stamp collections, and other contents of a jointly owned home may technically be regarded as the sole property of the deceased, but in everyday practice their ownership is often assumed informally by the surviving owner of the home unless some other person raises a claim. Thus, a surviving spouse informally assumes possession of the deceased's personal effects unless adult children or someone designated in the will lays claim to them—in which case the dispute may have to be resolved by the court after the commencement of probate proceedings.

In addition, some personal property, such as motor vehicles, personal effects, and unpaid salary, can be transferred informally under the laws of most states.

MOTOR VEHICLES

If the deceased's assets included boats or motor vehicles (not only passenger automobiles but also trucks, motor homes, recreational vehicles, and motorcycles), they may have been registered in his name alone. If their total value does not exceed a specified amount—usually between $25,000 and $75,000—ownership of these vehicles may be transferred to a surviving spouse or next of kin without the need for probate proceedings or help from a lawyer.

The local branch of your state motor vehicle bureau can tell you whether the simplified procedure is available and what it involves. Usually all the surviving spouse or other next of kin need do is present the vehicle title (which in some states is the current registration certificate) and a certified copy of the owner's death certificate. Once the applicant has signed an affidavit of heirship (provided by the motor vehicle bureau), title can be transferred into his or her name on payment of a nominal fee. The applicant's estimate of the vehicle's current value is not likely to be questioned, but reliable figures are available in several used-car guides available at banks, libraries, credit unions, and car dealerships.

If neither the spouse nor any other eligible next of kin transfers ownership of the deceased's vehicle, it becomes a probate asset and hence may require action by the probate court. To avoid this—especially if there are no other probate assets—it might be advisable for the spouse or other next of kin to have ownership of the vehicle transferred to his or her name and then to sell it immediately. If there are other probate assets, this tactic will have the effect of reducing their total value. In some states, however, this abbreviated transfer procedure is not available if probate administration of the estate is pending.

Of course, if the vehicle was owned jointly, ownership passes automatically to the surviving joint owner, as is the case with other jointly held assets. And if the vehicle title is held in a trust, it remains in the name of the trustee or successor trustee for disposition according to the terms of the trust document (see Chapter 12).

WAGES AND FRINGE BENEFITS

Any salary, wages, accumulated vacation and sick pay, and other fringe benefits owing to the deceased may, according to the laws of some states, be paid by the deceased's employer directly to the surviving spouse, adult children, or other next of kin without the need for any probate proceedings. The employer may, in order to protect his interests, require the claimant to first produce a death certificate and sign an affidavit that identifies him or her and specifies his or her priority right to receive the deceased's money.

The personnel departments of most large corporations are familiar with this procedure, but small employers may not be. If you encounter problems, consult your local probate court or the state department of labor. You should be able to collect the money without the help of a lawyer. If, however, you believe that the employer is withholding payment or is delaying it unreasonably, you might consider filing a complaint with the state department of labor, filing suit in small claims court, or, if the amount is substantial, retaining a lawyer.

TRAVELER'S CHECKS

Most issuers will redeem the deceased's unused traveler's checks without requiring the appointment of an executor or commencement of probate proceedings. The checks need merely be accompanied by a copy of the death certificate, an affidavit signed by the next of kin, and instructions as to who is to receive the refund.

"SMALL ESTATE" AND OTHER INFORMAL TRANSFER PROCEDURES

If the value of the deceased's probate assets does not exceed a certain amount, you may still be able to avoid formal probate administration. In response to public criticism of the probate process as antiquated, time-consuming, expensive, and designed to protect the job security of judges and lawyers rather than the interests of widows and orphans, most states have adopted streamlined, simplified, and relatively informal procedures for the transfer of certain "small estates." Many of these procedures do not require a lawyer, and most of them can be completed in a matter of hours or days, whereas formal probate administration often takes several months and, in some cases, may drag on for years.

Once you identify the deceased's probate assets, your first step is to find out —by consulting Tables 6.1 and 6.2, and inquiring of the local probate court, a local law library, or a lawyer skilled in probate law—precisely what the requirements are for "small estate" transfer procedures in the deceased's state of residence. If, instead, you simply approach a lawyer and ask him to "probate the estate," he or she may, knowingly or not, involve you in the full process of formal probate administration at a substantial cost to the survivors in both time and money.

As Tables 6.1 and 6.2 indicate, the eligibility of an estate for settlement by one of the "small estate" transfer procedures varies from one state to another, but generally it hinges on (1) the value of the assets, (2) the nature of the assets, (3) the relationship of the survivors to the deceased, and (4) whether or not the funeral bill has been paid. The two "small estate" transfer procedures described below, however, are sufficiently typical to serve as guidelines, although the precise requirements and procedures in the deceased's state of residence may differ in some respects from the general model.

TRANSFER BY AFFIDAVIT

For the transfer and settlement of "small estates"—usually defined as property not exceeding a specified maximum ($500 to $140,000)—many states offer an affidavit transfer procedure that eliminates the need for appointment of an executor, for probate-court administration, or for notification of the deceased's creditors. The transfer affidavit, usually a printed form available from the financial institution holding the deceased's money or other assets, must state (1) that the claimant is legally entitled to inherit the deceased's assets, (2) that the value of the entire estate, less liens, does not exceed the maximum permitted by state law, (3) that a minimum number of days (often 30 to 45) have elapsed since the death, and (4) that no petition for the appointment of an executor is pending or has been granted by a probate court. If the deceased left a will, some institutions may require a copy of it and will not release assets to anyone not designated as an entitled beneficiary.

Under the Uniform Probate Code (adopted by 16 states at the time of this writing), anyone indebted to or holding personal property of the deceased is required, on presentation of the transfer affidavit, to pay the debt or deliver the property to the person who claims to be an entitled beneficiary of the deceased. In simpler language, this means that the affidavit procedure can be used to collect and transfer the deceased's bank accounts, insurance policies, money market accounts, promissory notes, various securities, and the contents of safe deposit boxes—provided their total value falls within the state's specified monetary limits. Under this procedure, the deceased's creditors need not be notified or paid. Small estate transfer by affidavit usually cannot be used, however, for settling and distributing the deceased's real estate.

Other states, even though they have not adopted the Uniform Probate Code, provide similar procedures for the swift and informal transfer of "small estates" by affidavit. You may or may not need the help of a lawyer to take advantage of this shortcut. Before obligating yourself to legal expenses, however, find out what you can about your state's "small estate" affidavit transfer procedures by reviewing Table 6.1, calling the local probate court, or doing some research in a law library.

TABLE 6.1

Transfer of Small Estates by Affidavit

State	Dollar Limitation ($)	Waiting Period Following Death	Applicable to Real Estate	Creditors Must First Be Paid
Alabama		Not available		
Alaska[1]	15,000	30 days	No	No
Arizona[1]	50,000	30	No	No
Arkansas[1]	50,000	45	No	Yes
California	100,000	40	No	No
Colorado[1]	27,000	10	No	No
Connecticut[1]	20,000	30	No	No[6]
Delaware[1]	20,000	30	No	Yes
District of Columbia	2 cars	No	No	Yes
Florida		Not available		
Georgia		Not available		
Hawaii[1]	20,000	30	No	No
Idaho[1]	25,000	30	No	No
Illinois	25,000	No	No	Yes
Indiana[1]	25,000	45	No	No[6]
Iowa		Not available		
Kansas		Not available		
Kentucky		Not available		
Louisiana[3]	50,000	No	No	Yes
Maine[1]	10,000	30	No	No
Maryland	Formula[4]	No	No	No
Massachusetts	Formula[5]	60	No	No
Michigan[1]	15,000	28	No	No
Minnesota	20,000	30	No	No
Mississippi	20,000	30	No	No
Missouri	15,000	No	Yes	Yes
Montana[1]	7,500	30	No	No
Nebraska	25,000	30	No	No
Nevada	10,000	30	No	No

TABLE 6.1

Transfer of Small Estates by Affidavit *(continued)*

State	Dollar Limitation ($)	Waiting Period Following Death	Applicable to Real Estate	Creditors Must First Be Paid
New Hampshire[2, 7]	500	No	No	No
New Jersey[2, 3]	10,000	No	Yes	No
New Mexico[1]	20,000	30	No	No
New York	10,000	30	No	No
North Carolina[3]	20,000	30	No	Yes
North Dakota[1]	15,000	30	No	No
Ohio[7]	2,500	No	No	No
Oklahoma[1]	10,000	10	No	No
Oregon[3]	140,000	30	Yes	Yes
Pennsylvania		Not available		
Rhode Island	7,500	Not available		
South Carolina[1]	10,000	30	No	No
South Dakota	25,000	No	No	Yes
Tennessee	1,000	30	No	No[6]
Texas	50,000	30	Yes	No
Utah[1]	25,000	30	No	No
Vermont		Not available		
Virginia[1]	10,000	60	No	No
Washington[1]	60,000	40	No	Yes
West Virginia[1, 7]	1,000	120	No	No
Wisconsin	10,000	No	No	No
Wyoming[1]	70,000	30	No	Yes

[1] Not available if petition for appointment of personal representative has been granted or is pending.

[2] Available only if deceased is survived by a spouse.

[3] Available only if deceased left no will.

[4] Not more than two vehicles plus a boat (maximum value of $5,000) plus life insurance (maximum value of $1,000).

[5] Life insurance up to $10,000 plus bank accounts up to $3,000 plus wages up to $100.

[6] Funeral expenses must first be paid.

[7] Available only for wages, salaries, and commissions.

SUMMARY PROBATE ADMINISTRATION

If the deceased's probate assets exceed the maximum values specified by state law or do not consist of the types eligible for transfer
by affidavit, or if the assets include real estate, most states offer an
abbreviated form of probate procedure, sometimes called "summary" or "small estate" probate administration. This procedure is
usually available (1) if assets do not exceed a specified value, (2) if
no interested party (such as a creditor) objects to it, and (3) if the
will does not direct otherwise.

In California, for example, you may petition the probate court
to issue an order specifying the survivors' right to acquire the property without the need for full probate administration. The petition
must include an inventory and appraisal by a probate referee of the
deceased's real and personal probate property, showing its gross
value. The petition is scheduled for a hearing, and notice must be
given to all interested parties. If the petition is granted, the probate
court will issue an order specifying who acquires the title to the
property. A certified copy of this order is then delivered to the person or entity holding personal property and is recorded in the
county in which any real property is located.

The Uniform Probate Code also provides for summary probate
administration if the survivors include a spouse and minor children.
As the nominated executor, you may file an application for informal appointment and thereby obtain letters of authority (see p.
130). If, after you have filed an inventory and appraisal, it appears
that the value of the probate estate does not exceed the aggregate
value of (1) the statutory "family protection allowances" (approxi-
mately $25,000 but varying among states), (2) funeral expenses, (3)
necessary expenses for the deceased's final health care, and (4) costs
of administration, you may immediately distribute the estate to the
spouse and minor children without giving the normally required
notice to the deceased's creditors and opportunity for presentation
of their claims.

After the assets have been distributed, you can immediately
close the estate by filing a sworn statement that to the best of your
knowledge the value of the estate did not exceed the sum of items
1 through 4 above, that the distribution of assets is complete, and
that a copy of the final statement was sent to all beneficiaries and
to known unpaid creditors. Under this procedure, creditors need
not be paid.

TABLE 6.2
Summary Probate Requirements

State	Dollar Limitation ($)	Waiting Period Following Death	Applicable to Real Estate	Creditors Must Be Paid
Alabama	3,000	No	No	Yes
Alaska	Formula[2]	No	Yes	No
Arizona	Formula[2]	No	Yes	No
Arkansas	Formula[3]	No	Yes	No
California	100,000	No	Yes	No
Colorado	Formula[2]	No	Yes	No
Connecticut	Formula[2]	No	Yes	No
Delaware	Not available			
District of Columbia	15,000	No	Yes	No
Florida	60,000	No	Yes	Yes
Georgia	Not available			
Hawaii	20,000	No	Yes	No
Idaho	Formula[2]	No	Yes	No
Illinois[5]	50,000[4]	No	Yes	Yes
Indiana	Formula[2]	No	Yes	No
Iowa[6, 8]	50,000	No	Yes	Yes
Kansas	Formula[2]	6 mos.	Yes	Yes
Kentucky[5 or 7]	7,500	No	Yes	Yes
Louisiana	Not available			
Maine	Formula[2]	No	Yes	No
Maryland	20,000	No	No	No
Massachusetts[1]	15,000	30	No	No
Michigan	Formula[2]	No	Yes	No
Minnesota[1, 8]	30,000	No	Yes	No
Mississippi	500	No	No	No
Missouri	40,000	30	Yes	No
Montana	Formula[2]	No	Yes	No
Nebraska	Formula[2]	No	Yes	No
Nevada	200,000	60	Yes	Yes
New Hampshire	5,000	No	Yes	Yes

TABLE 6.2
Summary Probate Requirements *(continued)*

State	Dollar Limitation ($)	Waiting Period Following Death	Applicable to Real Estate	Creditors Must Be Paid
New Jersey		Not available		
New Mexico	Formula[2]	No	Yes	Yes
New York[8]	20,000	No	Yes	No
North Carolina		Not available		
North Dakota	Formula[2]	No	Yes	
Ohio	35,000	No	Yes	Yes
Oklahoma	60,000	No	Yes	Yes
Oregon	Formula[2]	No	Yes	Yes
Pennsylvania	25,000	No	No	No
Rhode Island	15,000	No	No	Yes
South Carolina[8]	10,000	No	Yes	No
South Dakota	60,000	No	Yes	Yes
Tennessee	10,000	45	Yes	
Texas	Formula[2]	No	Yes	Yes
Utah	Formula[2]	No	Yes	No
Vermont	10,000	No	No	Yes
Virginia	10,000	60	No	No
Washington		Not available		
West Virginia	100,000	No	Yes	No
Wisconsin[6]	30,000	No	Yes	Yes
Wyoming	70,000	No	Yes	Yes

[1] Not available if petition for appointment of personal representative has been granted or is pending.

[2] Available where entire estate, less liens and encumbrances, does not exceed certain statutory allowances plus expenses or last illness, funeral, and administration . . . all of which may approximate $25,000 in some cases.

[3] If personal property is less than statutory dower and allowances for widow or minors, court may immediately assign estate to them.

[4] Includes deceased's probate and nonprobate assets.

[5] Available only if all beneficiaries consent in writing.

[6] Available only if deceased is survived by a spouse, a child, or a parent.

[7] Available only if deceased is survived by a spouse.

[8] Available only if deceased left no will.

[9] Exclusive of statutory family allowances or exempt property.

FORMAL PROBATE ADMINISTRATION

If the value of the deceased's probate assets exceeds the maximum for your state's "small estate" transfer procedures, or if a lawsuit for wrongful-death benefits seems likely, the estate must undergo formal probate court administration.

Depending on the complexity of the probate assets, creditor claim disputes, will contests, disputes among the beneficiaries, and whether there is a delay in obtaining tax clearances, the probate process can take from six months to several years. And it will inevitably erode the value of the estate. Even if the deceased's will specified that you, as executor, would serve without bond and you agree to serve without fee, there will be court costs as well as expenses incurred for legal services, appraisals, and so on. Although formal probate administration might have been avoided if you had been able to convince the deceased to adopt some of the probate-avoidance strategies suggested in Chapter 3, it is, unfortunately, inevitable at this juncture.

The basic purposes of probate administration can help to explain why the process can be lengthy and costly. The court must appoint you as executor to identify, collect, and manage the deceased's probate assets and to settle the estate. It must determine the validity of any purported will and resolve disputes among beneficiaries. It must identify and notify the beneficiaries named in the will, as well as the heirs designated by state intestacy laws. It must supervise your responsibility to notify the deceased's creditors and determine the legitimacy of their claims. And it must ensure that the remaining assets, after taxes, debts, and administration expenses have been paid, are properly distributed by you to the will-designated beneficiaries or the heirs at law if the deceased left no will (see Chapter 11).

This rather complex process is the subject of the next three chapters.

～ 7 ～
INITIATING PROBATE

The administration of the deceased's probate assets by the probate court has several purposes. The court determines whether the will is valid. It appoints the executor and, if there are minor or incompetent survivors, a guardian and, in some cases, a conservator (an individual or institution capable of managing substantial assets). It supervises the management of the estate by the executor from the time of death to the ultimate distribution of the probate assets, and it ensures that taxing authorities and legitimate creditors of the estate will be paid. In short, it makes sure that everyone materially affected by the deceased's death will be treated in accordance with the will and the laws of the deceased's state of residence.

It is quite possible, however, that the estate for which you have been nominated executor will not require full probate administration. For one thing, the deceased's assets may have been left entirely in joint ownership or in a living trust, or may consist of life insurance not payable to the estate, or of accounts payable to beneficiaries designated by contract, in which case there are no probate assets—although these assets, as noted in Chapter 9, may nevertheless be subject to federal estate and state death taxes. For another, the value of the probate assets may be low enough to qualify for one of the "small estate" transfer procedures described in Chapter 6.

Having identified, collected, and appraised the deceased's assets as described in Chapter 5, you should be able to make a preliminary estimate as to whether probate administration can be avoided. If, however, a guardian or a conservator must be appointed for minor or incompetent survivors, probate-court intervention is inescapable. And probate administration is necessary, of course, if the value or type of the probate assets renders them ineligible for your state's small estate transfer procedures.

WHO INITIATES THE PROBATE PROCESS?

Since the will has nominated you as the executor, it is logical for you to file the petition to commence probate proceedings, especially if—as is often the case—you are a beneficiary. However, a petition may be filed by anyone who has an interest in the estate—will-designated beneficiaries, heirs at law, or creditors. The petition should not be filed unless, of course, the estate requires probate administration.

THE WILL

The deceased's will is crucial for commencement of probate, for several reasons. It may contain important evidence for determining where probate administration must take place. For example, if the opening paragraph of the will states, "I, John Jones, being a resident of the city of Seattle, state of Washington. . . .," probate may have to be conducted in the probate court of King County, where Seattle is located.

In addition, the will designates the deceased's beneficiaries, all of whom thus have an interest in commencing probate, if probate is necessary before they can collect their bequests.

Lastly, the will names an executor and may specify that the executor serve without fee or bond. Although the court is not obligated to appoint the testator's nominated executor, in most cases it does so.

Most states have laws requiring that the original will be filed with the probate court either immediately or within a short time (typically within 30 days after its discovery). In such states, neglecting or refusing to file the signed will can result in civil or criminal sanctions against anyone who withholds, secretes, or destroys it. But filing the will with the court does not in itself initiate probate administration of the deceased's estate because you may determine that probate is unnecessary for one of the reasons cited above. In such cases, the will simply remains on file with the court and probate administration is never commenced.

WILL YOU NEED A LAWYER?

Because the probate of an estate requires detailed knowledge of your state's probate, property, and creditor laws, local court rules, state death taxes, and possibly federal income, gift, and estate tax laws, you should probably retain a lawyer skilled in probate law. As we noted in Chapter 2, you, as the executor, could be subject to substantial personal liability for acts of both commission and omission. This is an additional reason for retaining an experienced probate lawyer.

If you plan to probate an estate by relying on your local probate register, clerk, or judge for advice, don't expect to receive much help. Many probate court offices display a prominent sign prohibiting court personnel from rendering legal advice. And even if you find a well-intentioned probate clerk who is willing to answer your questions on probate law, you have no right to rely on the validity of the answers. These clerks are not licensed lawyers, and no amount of "on the job" experience qualifies them to provide accurate legal advice.

Finding a skilled probate lawyer whose fees are reasonable may not be easy, but when you seek recommendations you should inquire about both issues: probate law experience and fees. The clerk of the probate court, the trust department of your local bank, and the chairperson of your local bar association or estate planning and probate council may be useful sources of recommendations. If you have acquaintances who have been involved with probating an estate, or if you know a local lawyer, ask them for recommendations.

The will that nominates you as executor may also specify the lawyer to be retained in settling the estate—sometimes the same lawyer who prepared the will. But as executor, you have the right to ignore this directive and to select a lawyer of your own choosing.

Once you have found a lawyer, you should discuss fees and expenses candidly, so as to get an estimate of the total fees and expenses involved in settling the estate. An hourly fee is usually preferable to a fee based on a percentage of the estate's value, provided that the rate is reasonable and that you are not charged the lawyer's rate for work performed by a paralegal or a student clerk. If the estate is not complex, you may be able to negotiate a lump-sum fee. In any event, once you have reached agreement on fees and expenses, ask the lawyer for a formal retainer contract or a letter confirming the agreement.

WHERE TO FILE PROBATE

Probate is undertaken in and governed by the state in which the deceased was domiciled—that is, the state in which the deceased maintained and intended to maintain a permanent residence. It is important to determine the deceased's state of domicile, because that state's laws control such issues as minimum requirements for a valid will, a surviving spouse's protection against disinheritance, and the rights of the deceased's creditors. In addition, the state of domicile has the right to impose inheritance or estate taxes and, if the issue is disputed, more than one state may attempt to impose these death taxes.

In many cases the state of domicile is easily determined—particularly if the deceased maintained only one dwelling and spent most of his time in one state. But residency questions can arise if the deceased maintained homes in more than one state or was in the process of moving from one state to another.

The issue of domicile hinges, in part, on where the deceased *intended* to maintain a permanent home. Thus, if the deceased spent part of the year in Michigan and part in Arizona, the issue of intention arises. This issue can be resolved by reference to several factors: the state where the deceased was registered to vote, the state that issued the driver's license and vehicle registration, the address used in employer records, and the address used by the IRS. As we have noted, the statement of residency contained in the will also constitutes important evidence.

Once the issue of domicile is resolved, probate administration is initiated in the country in which the deceased maintained a permanent residence.

ANCILLARY PROBATE

Although the petition for commencement of probate administration must be filed in the probate court in the county of the deceased's domicile, complications can arise if the deceased's probate assets include real property—such as a vacation home—in another state. Because the court in the county of the deceased's domicile has no jurisdiction over real property in another state, that "foreign" state requires separate court proceedings, called ancillary probate administration.

Generally the state in which the real property is located accepts the will admitted to probate in the deceased's state of domicile and issues to the executor letters of authority that permit the transfer of the property to the will-designated beneficiary or, if there is no will, to heirs at law. If the "foreign" state imposes inheritance or estate taxes, these taxes are payable to that state, and not to the state of the deceased's residence.

Ancillary probate will inevitably involve delay, finding and overseeing a reliable lawyer in another state, and additional expenses, including court costs and lawyers' fees. This fact alone is a compelling reason for out-of-state property to be owned jointly or by the trustee of a revocable living trust, in which case ancillary probate—and indeed, any probate—is avoided.

INITIATING PROBATE

Although a petition for commencement of probate proceedings can be filed by any interested party—including next of kin, a will-designated beneficiary, or a creditor—you, as the nominated executor, are the most likely person to file it, since you will know at the outset whether probate is required. This "petition for commencement of proceedings"—in some states called a "petition for probate of will"—is usually a printed legal form available from the probate court, an office supply firm, or a probate lawyer. A typical form is shown in Figure 7.1.

The content of the petition varies somewhat from one state to another, but typically it includes the following:

- A request that the will be admitted to probate
- Your interest in appointment as the executor
- Information about the deceased: name, date of death, age, and Social Security number
- The names and addresses of the deceased's spouse, children, and other heirs at law, the ages of any who are minors, and the identity of any who are legally incompetent
- The deceased's state of residence
- The date of the will and the names of its witnesses
- The estimated value of the probate assets

UNSUPERVISED ADMINISTRATION

Twenty-five states currently authorize the use of "unsupervised" (sometimes called "independent") probate administration, which lessens the amount of court supervision over the executor's administration of the estate. Originally permitted by the Uniform Probate Code, unsupervised administration is intended to simplify the executor's role and thus speed up the probate process.

Figure 7.1

STATE OF MICHIGAN PROBATE COURT COUNTY OF	PETITION FOR PROBATE AND/OR APPOINTMENT OF PERSONAL REPRESENTATIVE (TESTATE/INTESTATE)	FILE NO.

Estate of _____

1. I, _____, am interested in this estate and make this
   Name of petitioner

   petition as _____
   Relationship to decedent (i.e. heir, devisee, child, spouse, creditor, etc.)

   as defined by MCL 700.1105(c).

2. Decedent information: _____ _____m. _____
   Date of death   *Time (if known)*   *Age*

   _____ Domicile (at date of death) _____
   Social Sec. No.   *City/Township/Village*

   _____   _____
   County   *State*

   Estimated value of assets: Real estate $ _____

   Personal estate $ _____

3. So far as I know or could ascertain with reasonable diligence, the names
and addresses of the heirs and/or devisees of the decedent, the relationship
to the decedent, and the ages of any who are minors are as follows:

NAME	ADDRESS	RELATIONSHIP	AGE (if minor)

Of the above interested persons, the following are under legal disability or
otherwise represented and presently have or will require representation:

NAME	LEGAL DISABILITY	REPRESENTED BY Name, address, and capacity

Figure 7.1 *(continued)*

4. ❑ a. Venue is proper in this county because the decedent was domiciled in this county on the date of death.

❑ b. The decedent was not domiciled in Michigan, but venue is proper in this county because property of the decedent was located in this county at the date of death.

5. ❑ An application was previously filed and a personal representative was appointed informally.

PLEASE SEE OTHER SIDE

Do not write below this line - For court use only

---

6. ❑ A personal representative has been previously appointed in _____ County, _____ and the appointment has not
State

been terminated. The personal representative's name and address are:

_____   _____
Name   Address

_____
City, state, zip

7. ❑ The decedent's will, dated _____ , with codicil(s) dated _____ is offered for probate and is ❑ attached to this petition. ❑ already in the court's possession.

❑ An authenticated copy of the will and codicil(s), if any, probated in _____ County _____ is offered for
State

probate, and documents establishing its probate accompany this petition.

❑ Neither the original will nor an authenticated copy of a will probated in another jurisdiction accompanies the petition. The will is lost, destroyed, or otherwise unavailable, but its contents are: *(attach additional sheets as necessary)*

_____

8. ❑ The decedent's will was ❑ formally ❑ informally probated on _____ in _____ County.

9. To the best of my knowledge, I believe that the instrument(s) subject to this petition, if any, was validly executed and is the decedent's last will. After exercising reasonable diligence, I am unaware of an instrument revoking the will or codicil(s).

10. ❑ After exercising reasonable diligence, I am unaware of any unrevoked testamentary instrument relating to property located in this state as defined under MCL 700.1301.

Figure 7.1 *(continued)*

11. ❏ I nominate _____ , as personal represen-
Name

tative, who is qualified and has priority as: _____ .
His/her address is: _____
Address

_____ .
City, state, zip

Other persons having prior or equal right to appointment are:

_____   _____
Name   *Name*

_____   _____
Name   *Name*

12. ❏ The will expressly requests the personal representative serve with bond.

13. ❏ a. The decedent left a will that directs supervised administration.
     ❏ b. The decedent left a will that directs unsupervised administration, but supervised administration is necessary for the protection of persons interested in the estate because: (complete on line below)
     ❏ c. The decedent died intestate or left a will that does not direct supervised administration, but supervised administration is necessary because: (complete on lines below)

     _____

     _____

14. ❏ A special personal representative is necessary because

     _____

     _____

I REQUEST:

15. ❏ An order determining heirs and that the decedent died   ❏ testate.   ❏ intestate.

16. ❏ Formal appointment of the nominated personal representative ❏ with ❏ without   bond.

17. ❏ Supervised administration.

18. ❏ Appointment of a special personal representative pending the appointment of the nominated personal representative.

I declare under the penalties of perjury that this petition has been examined by me and that its contents are true to the best of my information, knowledge, and belief.

Figure 7.1 (continued)

	Date
Attorney signature	Petitioner signature
Attorney name (type or print) Bar no.	Petitioner name (type or print)
Address	Address
City, state, zip Telephone no.	City, state, zip Telephone no.

Some states allow unsupervised administration only if it is authorized in the will; others require the written consent of all interested persons. Still others permit the executor to commence unsupervised administration until such time as an interested person petitions the court to order traditional supervised probate administration.

Under unsupervised administration, an advance published notice is usually not required to open the estate, appoint the executor, or admit the will to probate. Similarly, unsupervised administration may avoid the need for advance court approval of the executor's proposed distribution, the executor's fee, and the final accounting. As we have noted above, however, use of unsupervised administration does not preclude any interested person from forcing the estate into supervised administration. The Uniform Probate Code allows any interested person to petition the court to require supervised administration over any aspect of the proceedings and thus require formal court hearings for appointing the executor, proving the will, approving executor and lawyer fees, and securing advance approval for other actions of the executor.

NOTIFYING INTERESTED PERSONS

In some states the court, in response to your petition, will set a hearing date some 30 to 45 days in the future. At this point, you must send to all interested persons (1) a copy of the petition and the will and (2) written notice specifying the time, date, and place of the hearing. At this hearing, the court, after listening to any interested persons, decides on the appointment of the executor, the amount of the bond (if any), and whether to admit the will to probate.

In other states, the nominated executor or some other inter-ested person files a petition for appointment, is appointed without advance notice to the interested persons, has the court set a hearing date for probate of the will, and then sends to all interested persons (1) notice of the executor's appointment, (2) a copy of the petition for probate of the will and a copy of the will, and (3) notice of the time, date, and place of the hearing on the petition to probate the will.

In either situation, the "interested persons" include not only the beneficiaries designated in the will but also the spouse, if any; all the deceased's next of kin who would have inherited the estate had there been no will; and all known creditors of the deceased.

This formal notification serves several purposes. It permits any interested person to file an objection to your appointment as execu-tor, to propose another candidate, and to seek to set aside any pre-liminary appointment. It affords an opportunity for any interested person to contest the will or its amendments. It allows a surviving spouse to choose between taking her bequest specified in the will or claiming her "elective share" of the estate (see p. 181) and claim-ing certain "family allowances" that are available in many states (see p. 182). And it protects the rights of "heirs at law"—people who are entitled to inherit in the absence of a valid will—should the court declare the purported will to be invalid (see Chapter 11).

In most cases, identifying and locating the "interested persons" is fairly simple, particularly when the deceased is survived by a spouse, parents, children, grandchildren, siblings, nieces, or nephews. But it can be troublesome if the deceased is not survived by any close relatives. You may be able to get help from the de-ceased's doctor, minister, rabbi, or priest, from persons who visited the funeral home and signed the guest register, or from friendly coworkers or neighbors. If the value of the estate is high, you may want to use the (expensive) services of a company that specializes in locating relatives through genealogical searches.

In addition to notifying beneficiaries and heirs at law, you as exec-utor are required to notify the deceased's creditors (see Chapter 8).

PROVING THE WILL

If the will has already been filed with the probate court, the court will release photocopies to anyone presenting proof of the deceased's death. If the will has not been filed, you are required to submit the original to the court along with your petition to commence probate proceedings. Unless it is waived by all interested persons, a hearing will be held, at which time the probate judge determines whether the purported will is legally sufficient and thus should be "admitted" as the deceased's last will and testament.

If a question arises as to the will's authenticity, testimony of one of the will's subscribing witnesses is usually sufficient to establish it. If neither an affidavit nor the testimony of a witness to the will is available, other evidence, such as the testimony of someone who is able to identify the testator's signature, may be used to prove valid execution of the will. In those states that allow use of a "self-proving" will, an affidavit included in the will suffices to prove its authenticity without the need to call a subscribing witness.

Once it has determined that the will was legally executed by the testator and was not subsequently revoked, the court will sign an order admitting the will to probate. At this point the terms of the admitted will govern several aspects of the probate proceedings, including appointment of the executor, any special powers granted to him, whether or not a bond is required, the appointment of guardians and conservators, the distribution of probate assets to the designated beneficiaries and any conditions imposed on the bequests, and the establishment of any trusts specified in the will.

CONTESTING THE WILL

No matter how carefully the will has been drafted, there always exists the possibility that it will be contested—usually by people who did not receive the inheritance they expected: disinherited spouses, alienated children, unwed cohabitants, or close friends who had been led to believe that they would be "remembered" by the deceased.

Grounds recognized for contesting a will include (1) that the deceased was mentally impaired when signing the will, (2) that the deceased was misled or defrauded—that is, that he signed what he thought was a document other than a will, (3) that undue influence overcame the testator's ability to make free choices when signing the will, (4) that the testator's purported signature on the will is a forgery, or (5) that the will failed to comply with state law as to witnesses or other statutory requirements governing its execution.

Anyone challenging the will has a heavy burden of proof to establish legal grounds for setting it aside, but if the court accepts the contestant's claim as valid, it will reject the entire will. The deceased will then be regarded as having died intestate and all probate assets (after debts and taxes have been paid) will be distributed to the "heirs at law" specified in the state's intestacy laws (see Chapter 10).

Will contests are resolved in one of several ways. First, the court may reject the contestant's attack on grounds that it lacks merit. Or the executor and the contestant may reach a compromise settlement in which the contestant receives something from the estate in return for withdrawing his challenge of the will. A final possibility is to have all challenges and defenses presented at a probate court trial which, depending on state law, may provide a right to a jury.

Although will contests are infrequent, they typically result in substantial legal expenses to the estate, a one- to three-year delay in closing the estate, and lifelong enmity among the litigants. You, as the executor, should therefore make every effort to settle a will contest promptly if it has legal merit and seems reasonable.

APPOINTMENT OF THE EXECUTOR

As we have noted, the probate court's first order of business is to appoint the executor. If a dispute arises over your appointment as the will-nominated executor, the court may appoint someone else. Although the priority varies from state to state, Table 7.1 indicates a typical order for the appointment.

TABLE 7.1

Typical Priority Order for Appointment of Executor

Priority Rank	Description of Candidates
1.	Persons named in will as executor and successor executor.
2.	Surviving spouse who is a will-designated beneficiary (or spouse's nominee).
3.	Other will-designated beneficiaries (or their nominee).
4.	Surviving spouse (or his/her nominee).
5.	Other heirs at law by degree of kinship (or their nominee).
6.	Any creditor 45 days after death.

On the other hand, you have the right to decline your appointment as executor. You may decide, for example, that you do not have the time, energy, patience, or skills necessary to administer the estate. Or perhaps you find the task too depressing, or you dislike the persons named as beneficiaries. If, however, you decline the appointment, you remain obligated to deliver to the probate court any original will in your possession. Upon receipt of your written declination, the court will appoint some other person or institution as executor.

There are, of course, equally good reasons for you to accept the appointment. For example, having loved and respected the deceased, you may wish to see the material aspects of his lifetime brought to a smooth and orderly conclusion. Or, if you are a beneficiary of the estate or any part of it, you may want to see that everything is done properly so that you receive your entitled inheritance promptly. Or you may simply be interested in earning the executor's fee to which you will be entitled.

Your initial decision to accept the appointment is not irrevocable. You may resign at any time after your appointment and before the closing of the estate. If you do so, however, you must account to the probate court for all the assets that you have collected, sold, and distributed up to the time of your resignation. It is also possible that you may die before the estate is settled and closed. In such circumstances, *your* estate's executor will file an accounting with the probate court, which, in turn, will appoint a successor executor.

Even if you do not resign, there is the possibility that, while you are serving, some interested person—beneficiary, heir at law, or creditor—will petition the court for your removal on the grounds of negligence, conflict of interest, undue delay in administering the estate, or, worse yet, embezzlement of the estate's assets. In such cases, a decision of the probate court to remove you terminates your involvement with the estate, although you will remain liable for any wrongful acts.

If you, as the will-nominated executor, decline the appointment, resign the position after appointment, or are removed, the court will appoint a successor executor. Ideally, the will should have named a person, a bank, or a trust company as successor executor. If not, the court will appoint one of its own choosing—usually in accordance with the order of priority shown in Table 7.1.

EXECUTOR'S FEES AND EXPENSES

Some wills specify that the executor is to serve without fee; others specify a fee in actual dollars. These provisions are not, however, sacrosanct. Unless there exists a separate contract, in most states you may, if you choose, seek a higher or lower fee. If you are also a beneficiary, you may waive the fee altogether so as to avoid payment of income tax and instead receive your entire share of the estate as an inheritance.

The executor's fee is usually set by state law, which generally allows "reasonable compensation" or sets the fee as a percentage of the estate's value (see Table 2.2). Furthermore, you are entitled to reimbursement from the estate for the expenses you incur, including those for professional assistance—from lawyers, appraisers, accountants, and others—in managing and settling the estate. In addition, you are entitled to pay, out of estate funds, lawyers' fees and other expenses incurred in the defense or prosecution of any proceeding involving the estate, such as a will contest or a dispute over a creditor's claim.

Probate courts continue to develop criteria for determining what is "reasonable compensation." These generally include the time and effort involved, the complexity and value of the estate, the skill needed to resolve issues and the results obtained, the executors' fees customarily charged in the locality, and the executor's experience and skill.

To protect beneficiaries against excessive fees and charges, the laws of most states permit any interested party to file objections and thus initiate a special court proceeding to determine whether the fees and expenses requested by an executor are reasonable. Upon request and advance notification of all interested persons, the court is empowered to review all your expenditures on behalf of the estate, to review your requested fee, and to require refunds to the estate if it determines that you have received excessive fees or unwarranted reimbursements.

BONDING THE EXECUTOR

A surety bond, obtainable from an insurance company, protects beneficiaries, heirs at law, and creditors from losses due to negligence or malfeasance by the executor. Although bonding is generally not required if the will states that you may serve without bond, interested persons may nevertheless request that you be bonded and the court may agree that bonding is desirable. In addition, the court may, on its own initiative, decide that bonding is necessary. On the other hand, even if a bond is required by the will, the court may decide that it is unnecessary.

Figure 7.2

STATE OF MICHIGAN PROBATE COURT COUNTY OF ___ CIRCUIT COURT - FAMILY DIVISION	BOND OF FIDUCIARY	FILE NO.

Estate of _____

1. The principal has been appointed _____ ,
 Type of fiduciary

accepts the duties of this appointment and, with the surety(ies), agrees to pay $ _____ to the State of Michigan as obligee for the benefit of the persons interested in the estate if the principal fails to discharge all duties according to law.

2. The surety(ies) agree to be jointly and severally liable on the bond with the principal and with each other.

3. The surety(ies) consent to the jurisdiction of the court that issued letters of authority to the principal in a proceeding pertaining to the principal's fiduciary duties.

4. If this is a bond for a special personal representative who is subsequently appointed personal representative, the obligations and liabilities of this bond remain in effect.

_____
Date

_____
Principal signature

_____	_____
Attorney name (type or print) Bar no.	*Principal name (type or print)*
_____	_____
Address	*Address*
_____	_____
City, state, zip Tel. no.	*City, state, zip Tel. no.*
_____	_____
Surety signature	*Surety signature*
_____	_____
Surety name (type or print)	*Surety name (type or print)*
_____	_____
Address	*Address*
_____	_____
City, state, zip Tel. no.	*City, state, zip Tel. no.*

Figure 7.2 *(continued)*

Oath of Personal Surety The surety acknowledges personal worth of the amount of the penalty in the bond over and above all debts and legal exemptions. Subscribed and sworn to before me on _____
Date

_____ County, Michigan.

My commission expires: _____
  Date

Signature: _____
    Notary public/deputy probate register

Do not write below this line - For court use only

I have examined and approve this bond.

_____   _____
  Date   *Judge/Probate register*   *Bar no.*

❑ No new letters of authority are to be issued.

If bonding is required by the court, you must purchase the bond and file it promptly, because failure to do so, usually within 30 days after notice that it is required, may constitute grounds for your nonappointment or your removal. And until the bond is obtained and filed, you should do nothing on behalf of the estate except what is necessary to preserve its assets.

The amount of the bond may be set by the terms of the will or by order of the court. Generally the amount is equal to the estimated value of probate assets consisting of personal property. As we have noted, the cost of the bond premium is payable from estate funds.

LETTERS OF AUTHORITY

Once the court has issued an order appointing you as executor, and once you have filed a statement of acceptance (and evidence of posting a surety bond if one is required), the court will issue you "letters of authority"—in some states called "letters testamentary." (For some obscure historical reason, the plural is used, even though the letters may consist of several copies of a single document.) This document serves as written notice to the world that you have been appointed and have full authority to act on behalf of the estate (see Figure 7.3).

Figure 7.3

STATE OF MICHIGAN PROBATE COURT COUNTY OF	LETTERS OF AUTHORITY FOR PERSONAL REPRESENTATIVE	FILE NO.

Estate of _____

TO: | *Name, address, and telephone no.*
|

You have been appointed and qualified as personal representative of the estate on _____ . You are authorized to do and perform all
              Date
acts authorized by law except as to the following:

❑ Real estate or ownership interests in a business entity excluded from your
    responsibilities in your acceptance of appointment

❑ Restrictions:

❑ These letters expire: _____
                    Date

_____   _____   _____
   Date   *Judge (formal proceedings)/Register (informal proceedings)*   *Bar no.*

SEE OTHER SIDE FOR NOTICE OF DUTIES.

_____
        Attorney name (type or print)   *Bar no.*

_____
                  Address

_____
       City, state. zip   *Telephone no.*

I certify that I have compared this copy with the original on file and that it is a correct copy of the original and that these letters are in full force and effect as of the date on the letters.

_____   _____
   Date   *Deputy register*

Do not write below this line - For court use only

Figure 7.3 *(continued)*

The following provisions are mandatory reporting duties specified in Michigan law and Michigan court rules and are not the only duties required of you. See MCL 700.3701 through MCL 700.3722 for other duties. Your failure to comply may result in the court suspending your powers and appointing a special fiduciary in your place. It may also result in your removal as fiduciary.

Duties for Supervised Administration

You are required to prepare and file with this court the following written reports.

INVENTORY: You are required to file with the probate court an inventory of the assets of the estate within 91 days of the date your letters of authority are issued or as ordered by the court. You must send a copy of the inventory to all presumptive distributees and all other interested persons who request it The inventory must list in reasonable detail all the property owned by the decedent at the time of death. Each listed item must indicate the fair market value at the time of the decedent's death and the type and amount of any encumbrance. If the value of any item has been obtained through an appraiser, the inventory should include the appraiser's name and address with the item or items appraised by that appraiser. [MCL 700.3706; MSA 27.13706, MCR 5.310(E)]

ACCOUNTS: You are required to file with this court once a year, either on the anniversary date your letters of authority were issued or on another date you choose (you must notify the court of this date) or more often if the court directs, a complete itemized accounting of your administration of the estate. This itemized accounting must show in detail all income and disbursements and the remaining property, together with the form of the property. Subsequent annual and final accountings must be filed within 56 days following the close of the accounting period. when the estate is ready for closing, you are also required to file a final account with a description of property remaining in the estate. All accounts must be served on the required persons at the same time they are filed with the court, along with proof of service.

CONTINUED ADMINISTRATION: If the estate is not settled within 1 year after your original appointment, you must file with the court and send to each interested person a notice that the estate remains under administration, specifying the reasons for the continued administration. You must give this notice within 28 days of the first anniversary of your appointment and all subsequent anniversaries during which the administration remains uncompleted. If such a notice is not received, an interested person may petition the court for a hearing on the necessity for continued administration or for closure of the estate.

Figure 7.3 *(continued)*

[MCL 700.3703(4); MSA 27.13703(4), MCL 700.3951(3); MSA 27.1395 (3), MCR 5.144, MCR 5.310]

ESTATE (OR INHERITANCE) TAX INFORMATION: You are required to submit to the court proof that no estate (or inheritance) taxes are due or that the estate (or inheritance) taxes have been paid. **Note:** The estate may be subject to inheritance tax.

CHANGE OF ADDRESS: You are required to inform the court and all interested persons of any change in your address within 7 days of the change.

| Duties for Unsupervised Administration |

You are required to prepare and provide to all interested persons the following written reports.

INVENTORY: You are required to prepare an inventory of the assets of the estate within 91 days from the date your letters of authority are issued and to send a copy of the inventory to all presumptive distributees and all other interested persons who request it. You are also required within 91 days from the date your letters of authority are issued, to file with the court the information necessary to calculate the probate inventory fee that you must pay to the probate court. You may use the original inventory for this purpose. [MCL 700.3706; MSA 27.13706, MCR 5.307]

CONTINUED ADMINISTRATION: If the estate is not settled within 1 year after your original appointment, you must file with the court and send to each interested person a notice that the estate remains under administration, specifying the reasons for the continued administration. You must give this notice within 28 days of the first anniversary of your appointment and all subsequent anniversaries during which the administration remains uncompleted. If such a notice is not received, an interested person may petition the court for a hearing on the necessity for continued administration or for closure of the estate. [MCL 700.3703(4); MSA 27.13703(4), MCL 700.3951(3); MSA27.1395(3), MCR 5.144, MCR 5.307]

ESTATE (OR INHERITANCE) TAX INFORMATION: You are required to submit to the court proof that no estate (or inheritance) taxes are due or that the estate (or inheritance) taxes have been paid. Note: The estate may be subject to inheritance tax.

CHANGE OF ADDRESS: You are required to inform the court and all interested persons of any change in your address within 7 days of the change.

You will need these letters in order to collect the deceased's probate assets. For example, in the absence of this document, a bank holding deposits in the deceased's name or a broker holding securities in the deceased's account will not release them to you. Similarly, if the deceased's real estate is to be sold, the buyer will not accept a deed signed by you unless it is accompanied by a copy of your letters of authority.

The number of copies of letters of authority you request will depend on the complexity of the deceased's assets. You will need one for each of the deceased's bank and brokerage accounts and for each parcel of real property. On the other hand, there is no point in obtaining too many, because they normally have a "shelf life" of only 12 to 15 months. Some securities firms and stock transfer agents will not accept letters more than 60 days old. If you encounter someone who refuses to accept an "outdated" copy, you can readily obtain updated copies from the clerk of the probate court.

COLLECTING AND SAFEGUARDING THE ASSETS

In most probate estates, the deceased's assets are relatively easy to identify. Generally they consist of furnishings, clothing, jewelry, money, securities, homes, or motor vehicles. Once you have been issued letters of authority, collecting these assets usually presents no problem, but some of them may be less obvious than others. One such asset is any legal claim that the deceased, if still alive, could assert, such as a claim against a physician for medical malpractice (see p. 94).

All nonliquid assets require appraisal. The value of most securities can be determined rather easily by consulting the *Wall Street Journal* stock and bond tables as of the date of the deceased's death. The value of real estate can be established by surveying selling prices for similar real estate in the same neighborhood, by using tax assessments, or by consulting a realtor or appraiser. Works of art, jewelry, and antiques may require the opinion of professional appraisers.

FILING AN INVENTORY

Once you have been appointed, you must file with the court (usually within 30 to 60 days of your appointment) a reasonably detailed inventory of the estate's probate assets, indicating the fair market value of each asset as well as any mortgages or liens out-

Figure 7.4

STATE OF MICHIGAN PROBATE COURT COUNTY OF CIRCUIT COURT - FAMILY DIVISION	INVENTORY	FILE NO.

In the matter of _____

I, _____ submit the following as a
Name (type or print)

complete and accurate inventory of all the assets of the estate and the fair market evaluations as of the:

❑ date of death (decedent's estate only).
❑ date of qualification as fiduciary (all other estates).

PERSONAL PROPERTY AND REAL ESTATE *(If property is encumbered, show nature and amount of lien)*	ESTATE'S INTEREST
TOTAL ASSETS	

PLEASE SEE OTHER SIDE

Do not write below this line - For court use only

Figure 7.4 *(continued)*

The following property has been appraised:

_____
Description of property

_____
Name of appraiser

_____
Address of appraiser

_____
City, state, zip

_____
Description of property

_____
Name of appraiser

_____
Address of appraiser

_____
City, state, zip

_____
Description of property

_____
Name of appraiser

_____
Address of appraiser

_____
City, state, zip

I declare, under penalty of perjury that this inventory has been examined by me and that its contents are true to the best of my information, knowledge, and belief.

_____
Date

_____   _____
Attorney signature   Signature

_____   _____
Attorney name (type or print)   Bar no.   Principal name (type or print)

_____   _____
Address   Address

_____   _____
City, state, zip   Tel. no.   City, state, zip   Tel. no.

standing against any of them. In addition, you are required to send a copy of this inventory to interested persons who specifically request it. Failure to comply with the inventory requirements can result in your removal as executor.

NEXT STEPS

Once you have received your letters of authority, you can collect all the deceased's probate assets, proceed to pay the deceased's taxes and lawful debts, and distribute the residue to the entitled beneficiaries. Until the assets are ultimately distributed, however, you are responsible for carefully protecting and managing them. These responsibilities are dealt with in Chapters 8 and 9.

≈ 8 ≈
CREDITORS' CLAIMS

As we have noted in Chapter 5, between the date of death and the final settlement of the estate, you must pay promptly many bills—taxes, insurance premiums, utility bills—that come due on property owned by the deceased, because failure to pay them could jeopardize the property. Failure to make mortgage payments on time, for example, may result in foreclosure. Failure to pay utility bills may result in damage to the property. (If necessary, you can pay these bills out of your own pocket and then be reimbursed from estate funds.) But your payments to other creditors need careful thought. Some survivors would like to see all debts paid promptly, so that the deceased will not be stigmatized for having died a debtor, but this is neither wise nor necessary. Although some unpaid debts may incur late charges, it is possible that some will not have to be paid at all.

Before paying any debts as they become due, you need to consider several factors. First, there may not be enough probate assets in the estate to satisfy the claims of all creditors, some of whom may not have priority standing. Second, the payment of illegitimate or tardy claims is not required at all, and payment of them may expose you to personal liability and removal from the executorship for improperly diminishing the estate's assets. Lastly, creditors' claims need not be paid if they are not submitted by a specified deadline.

TABLE 8.1
Time Limits for Submitting Creditors' Claims

State	
Alabama	6 months after issue of letters of authority or 5 months after creditor notice, whichever is later.
Alaska	4 months after publication of creditor notice.
Arizona	4 months after publication of creditor notice.
Arkansas	3 months after publication of creditor notice.
California	4 months after issue of letters of authority or 60 days after mailing of creditor notice.
Colorado	4 months after publication of creditor notice or 1 year after death, whichever is earlier.
Connecticut	3–12 months after publication of creditor notice, time to be set by court.
Delaware	8 months after death.
District of Columbia	6 months after publication of creditor notice.
Florida	3 months after publication of creditor notice.
Georgia	3 months after publication of creditor notice.
Hawaii	4 months after publication of creditor notice; if none, 3 years after death.
Idaho	4 months after publication of creditor notice; if none, 3 years after death.
Illinois	2 months after mailing of or creditor notice.
Indiana	5 months after publication of creditor notice.
Iowa	4 months after publication of creditor notice.
Kansas	4 months after publication of creditor notice.
Kentucky	6 months after issue of letters of authority.
Louisiana	Before or at final hearing.
Maine	4 months after publication of creditor notice.
Maryland	9 months after death or 2 months after mailing of creditor notice.
Massachusetts	4 months after executor posts bond.
Michigan	4 months after publication of creditor notice; if none, 3 years after death.

TABLE 8.1
Time Limits for Submitting Creditors' Claims *(continued)*

State	
Minnesota	3 months after publication of creditor notice.
Mississippi	3 months after publication of creditor notice.
Missouri	6 months after publication of creditor notice; if none, 3 years after death.
Montana	4 months after publication of creditor notice; if none, 3 years after death.
Nebraska	2 months after publication of creditor notice; if none, within 3 years of death.
Nevada	90 days after mailing of creditor notice; 60 days if estate is under $100,000.
New Hampshire	6 months after issue of letters of authority.
New Jersey	6 months after publication of creditor notice.
New Mexico	2 months after mailing of creditor notice; if none, 1 year after death.
New York	3 months after publication of creditor notice; if none, 7 months after issue of letters of authority.
North Carolina	90 days after mailing of creditor notice.
North Dakota	3 months after mailing of creditor notice; if none, 3 years after death.
Ohio	3 months after issue of letters of authority.
Oklahoma	2 months after mailing of creditor notice.
Oregon	4 months after publication of creditor notice.
Pennsylvania	1 year after death.
Rhode Island	6 months after publication of creditor notice.
South Carolina	8 months after publication of creditor notice.
South Dakota	4 months after publication of creditor notice, or 30 days after mailing of notice.
Tennessee	6 months after publication of creditor notice.
Texas	4 months after publication of creditor notice.
Utah	3 months after publication of creditor notice; if none, 1 year after death.
Vermont	4 months after publication of creditor notice; if none, 3 years after death.

TABLE 8.1

Time Limits for Submitting Creditors' Claims *(continued)*

State	
Virginia	1 year after publication of creditor notice.
Washington	4 months after publication of creditor notice.
West Virginia	90 days after publication of creditor notice
Wisconsin	3–4 months after publication of creditor notice (exact time set by court).
Wyoming	3 months after publication of creditor notice.

Except for taxes, debts are generally payable only from *probate* assets. This means that, with the notable exception of taxes, the proceeds of life insurance policies (unless the estate or its executor is named as the beneficiary) and assets owned jointly or held in a living trust or in some kind of payable-on-death account need not, in many states, be used to pay debts that were incurred by the deceased alone. And, no matter how close your relationship, you are under no legal obligation to pay the deceased's bills out of your own pocket—unless, of course, you and the deceased are joint debtors. If there are insufficient probate assets to pay all the creditors, some of them will simply be out of luck.

Some states, in order to prevent the estate from being completely depleted by creditors, guarantee a "family allowance" for a spouse or minor children that is exempt from creditors' claims. And estates eligible for settlement by "small estate" transfer procedures (see Chapter 6) are usually not required to pay unsecured debts.

Debts that are legally entitled to payment from the estate's assets include those incurred by the deceased alone as well as debts incurred jointly—on a joint credit card, for example. But joint debts need not be paid from the estate's assets if the surviving debtor pays them or if the creditor has not filed a claim against the estate within the state-specified claims period (see Table 8.1). If, however, joint debts are legitimate, and a claim is timely filed, you may want to pay them from estate assets if the surviving joint tenant is also the sole beneficiary.

Once creditors have been notified (see p. 143), they must submit their claims promptly, because no claims are enforceable against the estate if they are filed after expiration of the state-specified claims period.

INSURANCE FOR DEBTS

Your first step in carrying out your responsibilities for debt settlement is to check on whether the deceased had credit life insurance or other debt insurance that upon death will pay the unpaid balance on car loans, credit card charges, and other debts. In addition, mortgage life insurance may pay the entire balance due on mortgages. And health insurance may cover the deceased's last health care expenses. This step requires careful scrutiny of all the relevant documents, but it may produce a substantial saving of estate assets.

NOTIFICATION OF CREDITORS

When you assembled and collected the deceased's assets and liabilities (see Chapter 5), you became aware of the outstanding debts. Once you have obtained your letters of authority, your first formal step in settling the debts, therefore, is to notify all of the deceased's creditors who are known to you. But, because there may be creditors of whom you are not aware, you must also publish in a newspaper a notice of the probate proceedings and a general invitation to creditors to submit their claims within the state-specified claims period. If you publish this notice before receiving your letters of authority, it may be considered invalid and thus require republication.

Although state laws vary, many states require that the creditors' notice be published at least once in a newspaper having general circulation in the county in which the probate proceedings are held (see Figure 8.1). Typically, the creditors' notice must include the deceased's name, last address, date of death, and Social Security number. It must recite that the estate will be distributed to the persons entitled to it, and it must include your name as executor, your mailing address, and the address of the court. Many states require the notice to specify that a will has been admitted to probate or will be offered for admission, and to include the date of its execution. The notice must state that unless claims are submitted to you or to the court within a specified time (usually three to four months), they will be forever barred. The cost of publication is payable from estate funds.

Many states also require you to send a copy of the published notice to any creditor of the deceased who is known to you at the time of publication or becomes known to you within the claims period specified in the notice. You are deemed to have knowledge

Figure 8.1

STATE OF MICHIGAN PROBATE COURT COUNTY OF	NOTICE TO CREDITORS Decedent's Estate	FILE NO.

Estate of _____ Date of birth: _____
TO ALL CREDITORS:

NOTICE TO CREDITORS: The decedent, _____, who
lived at _____, Michigan
   Street address   *City*

died _____ .
 Date

Creditors of the decedent are notified that all claims against the estate will be forever barred unless presented to _____ , named personal representative or proposed personal representative, or to both the probate court at _____
    Address   *City*

and the named/proposed personal representative within 4 months after the date of publication of this notice.

_____
Date

_____ _____
Attorney name (type or print) Bar no. *Personal representative name (type or print)*

_____ _____
Address   *Address*

_____ _____
City, state, zip *Tel. no.* *City, state, zip* *Tel. no.*

PUBLISH ABOVE INFORMATION ONLY

Publish _____ time(s) in _____ in
    Name of publication

_____ County
Furnish _____ copies to _____
Furnish affidavit of publication to the probate court with copy to
_____

Forward statement for publication charges to _____

*NOTE TO PREPARER: If there is a known creditor whose address is unknown and cannot be ascertained after diligent inquiry, insert "including [name of creditor] whose address and whereabouts are unknown:"

Do not write below this line - For court use only

of a creditor if you are aware that the creditor demanded payment from the deceased while he was alive, or from the estate. You would be wise to publish the creditors' notice as promptly as possible so that you can start the running of the claims period and get an early indication of the number and amount of the claims that will be filed. Proof of publication must be filed with the court, usually in the form of an affidavit.

RESPONDING TO CREDITORS' CLAIMS

Every creditor's claim against the estate (see Figure 8.2) should be evaluated to determine its validity. Objections to claims may be filed by you or by any interested persons who stand to lose if an invalid claim is paid—for example, beneficiaries, heirs at law, or other creditors.

Objections to claims must be filed within a specified period— usually three to four months—or within a specified number of days following submission of the claim, whichever is later. Objections may be filed on the grounds that the debt was previously paid, that the goods or services were never received or that they were of sub-standard quality, that the statute of limitations renders the claim unenforceable, or that the claim was submitted after the claims deadline had passed.

Objections should not be filed frivolously. If, for example, you feel that a claim has merit but that the amount is excessive, discussion with the creditor may be far less time-consuming and more effective than filing an objection.

If an objection is to be filed, it must also be sent by registered mail to the creditor, and a copy filed with the court. The objection must identify the objector's interest in the estate, identify the objectionable claim, and specify the reasons for the objection. The claimant has a limited time (usually 30 days) within which to respond. If no response is received, the claim is barred. If, on the other hand, the claimant does respond, the court will hold a hearing, receive evidence, and determine whether the claim should be allowed (in whole or in part) or disallowed.

PAYMENT OF ALLOWED CLAIMS

Claims presented within the specified claims period and not objected to in a timely fashion may be paid at the expiration of the deadline. Contested claims may be paid only to the extent that the

Figure 8.2

STATE OF MICHIGAN PROBATE COURT COUNTY OF CIRCUIT COURT - FAMILY DIVISION	STATEMENT AND PROOF OF CLAIM	FILE NO.

Estate of _____

I, _____ submit the following
Creditor's name
claim against the estate for the sum set forth.*

DESCRIPTION OF CLAIM	AMOUNT
There is now due on the claim above all legal set-offs, the sum of:	

❏ Notice to interested persons: This is a claim by a personal representative for an obligation that arose before the death of the decedent. A hearing will be held to determine whether to allow the claim. You may object to the claim before or at the hearing.

I declare under penalties of perjury that this statement and proof of claim has been examined by me and that its contents are true to the best of my information, knowledge, and belief.

_____	_____
Attorney signature	*Date*
_____	_____
Name (type or print) *Bar no.*	*Claimant signature*
_____	_____
Address	*Address*
_____	_____
City, state, zip *Tel. no.*	*City, state, zip* *Tel. no*

*1. Describe nature of claim or attach statement. Attach copy of receipt or other evidence of payment if submitted by assignee.

Figure 8.2 (continued)

---

2. Claims must be presented either personally or by mail to the fiduciary on or before the last day for presentment of claims. This claim may also be filed with the probate court (see reverse side for proof of service).

PLEASE SEE OTHER SIDE

Do not write below this line - For court use only

PROOF OF SERVICE

I served upon _____, fiduciary, a
Name

copy of this statement and proof of claim on _____ by
Date

_____ .
State manner and address of service

I declare under the penalties of perjury that this proof of service has been examined by me and that its contents are true to the best of my information, knowledge, and belief.

_____   _____
Date   *Signature*

ACKNOWLEDGEMENT OF SERVICE

Service of the attached statement and proof of claim is acknowledged.

_____   _____
Date   *Signature*

---

court allows payment. No claim should be paid before the expiration of the claims deadline, and usually no interest charges are permitted until the expiration of the deadline.

If there are debts of which you are aware even though no claim has been filed, you are entitled to pay them provided you obtain the consent of all interested persons. If, as executor, you pay a claim that does not comply with the applicable claims law, you do so at your own risk. If such a claim is subsequently disallowed on objection by an interested person, you may be required to reimburse the estate personally. Of course, if you are the sole beneficiary and there are ample estate funds, you can pay whatever claims you choose since payment is, in reality, coming out of your own pocket.

PRIORITY CLAIMS

If there are not enough probate assets in the estate to pay all the allowed claims, state law establishes an order of priority of payment. Although this order varies from one state to another, the following is typical.

1. Costs and expenses of administering the estate, including the executor's fees and bond premiums, lawyer fees, and any other professional assistance that the executor needed, and court costs.
2. Reasonable funeral and burial expenses.
3. Federal taxes.
4. Reasonable and necessary medical and hospital charges incurred by the deceased immediately before death.
5. State taxes.
6. All other claims.

Under this priority system, high-priority claims are paid in full and, if there are no remaining assets, low-priority creditors get nothing. If, for example, after paying all debts in categories 1 through 5, the estate remains with $500 in assets and $1,000 in debts, each class 6 creditor will receive only 50 percent of his claim.

PAYMENT OF CLAIMS

On the expiration of the claims period provided in the notice to creditors, you are expected to pay all the allowed claims. These should be paid promptly, because delay may cause late-payment and interest charges to accrue. If the assets are insufficient to pay all the debts in full, payment should be made according to the priority governing claims noted above. Payment should be made by check from the estate's account (see Chapter 5).

Although your primary source of funds for paying the allowed claims will be the funds you have accumulated in the estate's checking account, you may have to sell some nonliquid probate assets—such as securities, real estate, and collectibles—in order to generate funds sufficient to pay all allowed claims.

Your basic guide as to which assets to liquidate and which to preserve is the will. If the will makes no provision, state law may provide an order of priority in reducing gifts made in the will in order to pay the allowed claims. Gifts specified in the will's residuary clause are usually the first to be liquidated. If these are not sufficient, general money bequests—that is, bequests of a dollar amount but not from a specified source—are reduced, or eliminated entirely if necessary, followed by the dollar bequests payable from specified sources—that is, from named assets, such as securities. A bequest of specific property—whether real or personal—may be liquidated only as a last resort.

In determining what to sell and what to retain, you may want to consult the beneficiaries, because a consensus among them can provide you with the answer. Alternatively, you may want to consult a probate lawyer, although if probate administration is pending, you may need the approval of the court.

TAXES

In many cases, the most onerous (but also most important) of the executor's responsibilities involves the payment of state and federal taxes on behalf of the deceased and, in some cases, on behalf of the estate itself. If the value of the estate is high or the probate process complicated, you should probably enlist the services of a certified public accountant or a tax lawyer unless, of course, you possess the necessary skills. Even if you use outside help, however, you as the executor remain personally responsible for the timely filing of returns and the payment of all taxes. Late returns and tax payments will not be excused on the grounds that the delay was caused by the professionals you retained.

Both income tax and federal estate tax are regarded as "debts," and they take priority over most all other creditor claims. If there is insufficient money in the probate estate to pay all creditors, the United States government must be paid before most other creditors. If you were aware of the deceased's and the estate's tax obligations and neglected to pay them before you distributed the assets to the beneficiaries, you can be held personally liable for the taxes owed up to the amount that you distributed.

The taxes you will be required to pay will depend on the value of the estate, the deceased's and the estate's taxable income, and on state laws regarding estate and inheritance taxes. It is not likely that you will have to pay all the taxes listed below, but we will deal with each of them in some detail to keep you from overlooking any and to allow you to check on the work of any professionals you employ.

You may be required to pay the following taxes.

For the deceased:
Final federal income tax (Form 1040);
Final state and local income tax if required by the deceased's state of residence.

For the estate:
Federal income tax for the estate if the gross income of the estate is $600 or more;
State income tax for the estate if required by the deceased's state of residence;
Federal estate tax if the value of the deceased's taxable estate exceeds $675,000[1];
State inheritance or estate tax if required by the deceased's state of residence.

Each of these taxes will be dealt with separately, but specific dollar amounts will not be given since they are subject to change.

FEDERAL INCOME TAX ON THE DECEASED

The deceased's final income tax return is due at the same time as it would have been due had the deceased not died—usually April 15 regardless of the date of death—and it must account for all taxable income earned to the date of death. In addition, you must file any returns due but not filed for preceding years. The return can be filed in whichever of the following categories is most appropriate with respect to the deceased's age and status:

Married, filing jointly
Married, filing separately
Single
Head of household
Qualifying widow(er)
Self-employment income

Even if the deceased had no taxable income for the tax year, a return must be filed if the deceased owed any taxes (for example, Social Security or Medicare taxes) or to obtain a refund of over-payment of withholding or estimated income taxes.

When filing any return for the deceased, the form should include the word "Deceased," followed by the deceased's name,

---

[1] The estate-tax exclusion amount, which is $675,000 for deaths in years 2000 and 2001, is indexed for inflation until 2006, when it reaches $1 million (see Table 9.2, p.164).

address, and date of death and (if the return is joint) the name and address of the surviving spouse. Whether or not the return is joint, you must sign it as the executor.

The deceased's final federal income tax return must be filed for the year in which the deceased died. The period that the return covers extends from the beginning of the taxable year to the date of death and is due on the date when the deceased would have paid the tax had he lived. Thus, if the deceased followed a calendar year for payment of income taxes and died on April 1, 2001, his last taxable year would extend from January 1, 2001, to the date of his death and the return would be due on April 15, 2001.

An automatic extension is available on the filing of Form 4868, but this extension does not extend the time for actual payment of the tax due. If the tax is not paid when the application is filed, interest will be charged at 0.5 percent per month unless at least 90 percent of the actual tax liability was paid prior to the due date through estimated payments, withholding, or payment submitted with the Form 4868.

If the deceased's series taxable year is short, there may be no need to file a return. For example, if the deceased died on January 15, his final tax obligation may not reach the minimum required for filing. If, however, the deceased's estate may be entitled to a refund for excess taxes withheld from salary or wages, you should file a return and include Form 1310, "Statement of Person Claiming Refund Due a Deceased Taxpayer" together with a copy of your letters of authority.

If the deceased is survived by a spouse, you, as executor, have the choice of filing a joint return with the spouse or filing a separate return for the deceased. Filing a joint return may produce substantial tax savings if it permits the surviving spouse to offset income received after the deceased's death against large deductions claimed by the deceased. These deductions might otherwise be lost if the deceased did not have enough income to take advantage of them.

The executor may not file a joint return if (1) the surviving spouse remarries during the deceased's taxable year, (2) either spouse was a nonresident alien during the deceased's taxable year, or (3) either spouse had a short taxable year by virtue of a change in the accounting period.

The filing of a joint return requires the assent of both the executor and the surviving spouse. But the surviving spouse may make the decision unilaterally if (1) the deceased has not already filed a return for the taxable year, (2) no executor has been appointed by the time the joint return is made, and (3) no executor has been appointed before the due date for filing the surviving spouse's return.

Filing a Joint Return

As the executor, you are responsible for the filing of a joint return unless the return is filed before you have been appointed, in which case the surviving spouse can file it and sign the return "filing as surviving spouse." But a joint return may not be filed by the surviving spouse who remarries before the end of the year of the deceased's death. In such circumstances, the status of the deceased's return must be "married filing separately."

A surviving spouse who files a joint return qualifies for special tax rates for the two years following the death of the first spouse— a fact that you need to be aware of if the deceased left a surviving spouse.

Exemptions and Deductions

In general, the deductions allowed on the deceased's return are the same as those allowed on any return, but under certain conditions the medical expenses that exceed 7.5 percent of the adjusted gross income can be taken as deductions *either* from the income tax return or from the federal estate tax but not from both. Because most decedents pay no federal estate tax this choice is likely to be meaningless. It may be useful for some, however, because the federal estate tax bracket is invariably higher than the deceased's income tax bracket.

Interest on the deceased's Series E or EE bonds was not reportable until the bonds were redeemed. A taxpayer could, however, elect to report the income as it accrues. If you elect to report the interest, then all interest previously deferred must also be reported. Such an election may be used to absorb deductions if the deceased had large deductions but little income. In addition, any income tax paid on the accrued interest is deductible as an expense for estate tax purposes.

The handling of medical expenses also offers an option. The deductible amount (beyond 7.5 percent of adjusted gross income) may be taken as medical expenses on the estate tax return or on the income tax return or divided between these two taxes. However, the deduction of medical expenses on the estate tax is not reduced by the 7.5 percent adjustment out of gross income. When deciding how to allocate the medical expense deduction, you should bear in mind that if the estate is subject to an unlimited marital deduction, an estate tax deduction for medical expenses would be wasted.

STATE AND LOCAL INCOME TAX

If the deceased's state or city of residence imposes an income tax, you may need to file a state or local return. State and local laws should be consulted to determine the filing requirements, the taxes due, and the responsibility for filing the return and paying the tax.

FEDERAL INCOME TAX ON THE ESTATE

If the probate assets do not earn income during probate adminis-tration of the estate, or if the income they earn (in dividends, inter-est, or rents, for example) amounts to less than $600, there is no need for you to file a federal income tax return on behalf of the estate unless one or more of the beneficiaries are nonresident aliens. But because large estates are likely to produce income, especially when probate administration takes a long time, you need to con-sider the possibility that the estate as a separate entity will be liable for tax on all income earned by estate assets between the date of death and the final distribution of the assets. If a tax is owed but not paid before distribution is made to the beneficiaries, they will become personally liable for it in proportion to their distributed share of the estate.

Your first step as executor is to complete IRS Form SS-4, Appli-cation for an Employer Identification Number, obtainable from your nearest post office or Social Security office. This number serves many of the same purposes as a personal Social Security number. You will need to enter it on tax returns, statements, and other documents you file on behalf of the estate. You will also need to provide this number to payers of interest, dividends, and other monies, who must file a Form 1099 in connection with income earned by the estate. Failure to include the Employer Identification Number on any tax return will make you liable for a penalty of up to $50 for each failure unless you can establish reasonable cause for this omission.

The estate income tax, reported on IRS Form 1041, is generally computed on the same basis as for individuals, subject to certain

TABLE 9.1
State Individual Income Tax Rates
(As of December 31, 1998)

	Federal Deduct-ibility	Marginal Rates (a) (Percent)	No. of Brackets	Low Bracket (a) (b) (Under)	High Bracket (a) (b) (Over)	Standard Deduction		Personal Exemptions	
						Single	Joint	Single (b)	Dependents
Alabama	Yes	2.0–5.0%	3	$ 500	$ 3,000	$ 2,000	$ 4,000	$ 1,500	$ 300
Alaska	No	None	n.a.	n.a.	n.a.	n.a.	n.a.	n.a.	n.a.
Arizona	No	2.9–5.1	5	150,000		3,600	7,200	2,100	2,300
Arkansas	No	1.0–7.0 (l)	6	3,000	25,000	2,000	4,000	20 (c)	20 (c)
California	No	1.0–9.3	6	5,131	33,673	2,642	5,284	70	70 (c)
Colorado	No	——5% of federal taxable income——				n.a.	n.a.	n.a.	n.a.
Connecticut	No	3.0–4.5	2	7,500	7,500	n.a.	n.a.	12,000 (e)	0
Delaware	No	0.0–6.9	7	2,000	30,000	1,300	1,600	100 (c)	100 (c)
Florida	No	None	n.a.	n.a.	n.a.	n.a.	n.a.	n.a.	n.a.
Georgia	No	1.0–6.0	6	750	7,000	2,300	3,000	2,700	2,700
Hawaii	No	2.0–10.0	8	1,500	20,500	1,500	1,900	1,040	1,040
Idaho	No	2.0–8.2	8	1,000	20,000	4,250	7,100	2,700	2,700
Illinois	No	3.0	1	n.a.	n.a.	n.a.	n.a.	1,300	1,300
Indiana	No	3.4	1	n.a.	n.a.	n.a.	n.a.	1,000	1,000
Iowa	Yes	0.36–8.98	9	1,136	51,120	1,440	3,550	40 (c)	40 (c)

State									
Kansas	No	3.5–6.45	3	15,000	30,000	3,000	6,000	2,250	2,250
Kentucky	No	2.0–6.0	5	3,000	8,000	1,200	1,200	20 (c)	20 (c)
Louisiana	Yes	2.0–6.0	3	10,000	50,000	n.a.	n.a.	4500 (m)	1,000
Maine	No	2.0–8.5	4	4,150	16,500	4,250	7,100	2,400	2,400
Maryland	No	2.0–4.875	4	3,000	2 000 (n)	4000 (n)	1,750	1,750	
Massachusetts	No	5.95/12.0 (f)	1	n.a.	n.a.	n.a.	n.a.	4,780	1,000
Michigan	No	4.4	1	n.a.	n.a.	n.a.	n.a.	2,800	2,800
Minnesota	No	6.0–8.5	3	16,960 (o)	55,730 (o)	4,250	7,100	2,700	2,700
Mississippi	No	3.0–5.0	3	5,000	10,000	2,300	3,400	6,000	1,500
Missouri	Yes	1.5–6.0	10	1,000	9,000	4,250	7,100	1,200	1,200
Montana	Yes (p)	2.0–11.0	10	2,000	69,000	2,960 (p)	5,920 (p)	1,580	1,580
Nebraska	No	2.51–6.68	4	2,400	26,500	4,250	7,100	88 (c) (q)	88 (c) (q)
Nevada	No	None	n.a.	n.a.	n.a.	n.a.	n.a.	n.a.	n.a.
New Hampshire	No	5.0 (h)	n.a.	n.a.	n.a.	n.a.	n.a.	2,400	n.a.
New Jersey	No	1.4–6.37	6	20,000	75,000	n.a.	n.a.	1,000	1,500
New Mexico	No	1.7–8.5%	7	$ 5,500	$ 65,000	$ 4,250	$ 7,100	$ 2,700	$ 2,700
New York	No	4.0–6.85	4	20,000	7,500	13,000	n.a.	1,000	
North Carolina	No	6.0–7.75	3	12,750	60,000	3,000	5,000	2,700 (r)	2,700 (r)
North Dakota	Yes (d)	—	—	——14% of federal income tax liability——		n.a.	n.a.	n.a.	n.a.
Ohio	No	0.673–6.79	9	95,000	200,000	n.a.	n.a.	950 (g)	1050 (g)
Oklahoma	Yes (d)	0.5–7.0	8	1,000	10,000	2,000 (s)	2,000 (s)	1,000	1,000

TABLE 9.1
State Individual Income Tax Rates (continued)
(As of December 31, 1998)

	Federal Deduct-ibility	Marginal Rates (a) (Percent)	No. of Brackets	Low Bracket (a) (b) (Under)	High Bracket (a) (b) (Over)	Standard Deduction		Personal Exemptions	
						Single	Joint	Single (b)	Dependents
Oregon	Yes	5.0–9.0	3	2,300	5,800	1,800	3,000	132 (c)	132 (c)
Pennsylvania	No	2.8	1	n.a.	n.a.	n.a.	n.a.	n.a.	n.a.
Rhode Island	No	——27% of federal income tax liability——				n.a.	n.a.	n.a.	n.a.
South Carolina	No	2.5–7.0	6	2,3101	1,550	4,250	7,100	2,700	2,700
South Dakota	No	None	n.a.	n.a.	n.a.	n.a.	n.a.	n .a.	n.a.
Tennessee	No	6.0 (h)	n.a.	n.a.	n.a.	n.a.	n.a.	n.a.	n.a.
Texas	No	None	n.a.	n.a.	n.a.	n.a.	n.a.	n.a.	n.a.
Utah	Yes	2.3–7.0	6	750	3,750	4,250	7,100	2,025	2,025
Vermont	No	——25% of federal income tax liability——				n.a.	n.a.	n.a.	n.a.
Virginia	No	2.0–5.7	5	43,000	17,000	3,000	5,000	800	800
Washington	No	None	n.a.	n.a.	n.a.	n.a.	n.a.	n.a.	n.a.
West Virginia	No	3.0–6.5	5	10,000 (i)	60,000 (i)	n.a.	n.a.	2,000	2,000
Wisconsin	No	4.77–6.77	3	7,500 (j)	15,000 (j)	5,200 (k)	8,900 (k)	0	50
Wyoming	No	None	n.a.	n.a.	n.a.	n.a.	n.a.	n.a.	n.a.
Dist. of Columbia	No	6.0–9.5	3	10,000	20,000	2,000	2,000	1,370	1,370

(a) Applies to single taxpayers and married people filing separately.

(b) Except for Delaware and Mississippi, married-joint filers receive double the single exemption. Delaware is a flat $100 tax credit and Mississippi is $9,500 for joint.

(c) Tax credit.

(d) Rates listed assume that taxpayers opt not to deduct their federal income tax liability. In North Dakota a filer who chooses to deduct his federal liability faces a range of rates from 2.6%–12% or income up to $3,000 and over $50,000, respectively. In Oklahoma, if a filer chooses to deduct his federal liability, then he faces a range of rates from 0.5%–10% on income up to $1,000 and over $16,000 respectively.

(e) Taxpayers receive a declining tax credit instead of a deduction or exemption. For Connecticut, the credit is 75% of tax liability starting at $14,000 of taxable income and declines to 0% after $52,000.

(f) The 12% rate applies to interest, dividends and capital gains.

(g) Taxpayers receive an extra $20 tax credit per exemption.

(h) Applies to interest and dividend income only

(i) For married filing separately, the low and high brackets are $5,000 and $30,000.

(j) For married filing separately, the low and high brackets are $5,000 and $10,000

(k) Deduction phases out to zero for single filers at $51,000 and joint filers at $55,000.

(l) Rates apply to regular tax table. A special tax table is available for low-income taxpayers that reduces their tax payments.

(m) Standard deduction and personal exemptions are combined: $4,500 for single and married filing separately; $9,000 married filing jointly and head of household.

(n) The standard deduction is taken as a percent of income (15 percent) and capped at $2,000 for single filers, married filing separately filers and dependent filers earning more than $13,333. The standard deduction is capped at $4,000 for married filing jointly filers, head of household filers and qualifying widowers earning more than $26,667.

(o) For married, filing separately, the low bracket is $12,400 and the high bracket is $49,270.

(p) Can claim either the standard deduction or the amount of federal taxes withheld—whichever is greater.

(q) The $88 personal exemption credit is phased out for filers with adjusted gross income of $62,000 or more.

(r) Exemptions are based on federal standards deductions but are adjusted according to income and filing status.

(s) The deduction given is applicable to all filers, excluding married filing separately filers, with adjusted gross income (AGI) over $13,333. For those with AGI between $6,666 and $13,333 the standard deduction is 15% of AGI and for those with AGI of less than $6,666 the standard deduction is $1,000. For married filing separately filers, the standard deduction is $500 or 15% of AGI, but not to exceed $1,000.

Sources: Respective state tax forms and instructions, Commerce Clearing House, Federation of Tax Administrators.

differences in computing deductions and credits. Taxable income includes dividends, interest, rents, royalties, profits from the sale of property, and income from a business, partnership, trust, or any other source. The estate is allowed an exemption of $600 but no exemption for dependents. The cost of administering the estate can be deducted from the gross estate, either on the estate's income tax return (see p. 155) or on the federal estate tax return (see p. 161) but not on both.

Medical and dental expenses of the deceased are not deductible on the estate's income tax return but, if paid within a year of the death, can be deducted on the deceased's final individual income tax return. Funeral expenses can be deducted only on the federal estate tax return, not on the individual or estate income tax return.

If your duties as executor include operation of the deceased's business, you should consult IRS Publication 334, *Tax Guide for Small Business*, which explains the applicable tax and employment laws.

The estate's income tax return is your responsibility and, like the deceased's individual return, it must be filed annually, on either a calendar or a fiscal-year basis. The fiscal year can be any period that ends on the last day of any month and does not exceed 12 months. As executor, you can choose the fiscal period when you file the estate's first income tax return. The estate's income tax liability must be paid in full when the return is filed. Estates with tax years ending two or more years after the date of death must pay estimated tax just as individuals do. If you are required to make estimated tax payments, use IRS Form 1041ES, Estimated Income Tax for Fiduciaries, to determine the estimated tax due. In filing Form 1041, enter the name of the estate exactly as it appears on the Employer Identification Number form. In the remaining spaces enter your name and address as the estate's executor.

STATE AND LOCAL ESTATE INCOME TAX

If the deceased's state, county, or city of residence imposes an income tax, you may need to file a state or local return. State and local law should be consulted to determine the filing requirements, the taxes due, and the responsibility for filing the return and paying the tax.

FEDERAL ESTATE TAX

The federal estate tax applies only to estates with a value exceeding $675,000[1] as of the date of death. Hence, if the estate for which you are the executor does not approach this value, you have no need to read this section. Before skipping it, however, you must bear in mind that this value is not computed on the basis of *probate* assets alone. It includes not only solely owned (probate) assets but also all assets in which the deceased had an interest at the time of death, including

  jointly owned assets;
  life insurance proceeds;
  assets held in the deceased's revocable living trust;
  assets held in the deceased's accounts which designate a pay-
    on-death or transfer-on-death beneficiary.
  certain gifts made within three years of death or taking effect
    at death;
  custodial accounts for minors for which the deceased was the
    donor and died while serving as custodian;
  the deceased's half-interest in any community property.

For purposes of computing the tax, the total value of these assets can be determined either as of the date of death or, alternatively, six months thereafter.

The estate tax return (IRS Form 706) is due within nine months of the date of death, and it is your responsibility as executor to file it and pay any tax due. If it is impossible or impractical for you to file within this time limit, the IRS may grant you an extension—usually no more than six months—but this extension does not allow you to postpone payment of the tax at the time it is due. Your application for the time extension must be accompanied by payment of the estimated estate tax.

An extension may be granted for any of the following reasons:

Reasonable cause: up to one year when, for example, the estate's assets lie in several jurisdictions, including the right *to* receive future payments or a claim that must be litigated or are insufficient to pay the tax.

Undue hardship: up to ten years if, for example, the estate consists of a closely held business that is not eligible for Internal Rev-

---

[1] The estate tax exclusion amount, which is $675,000 for deaths during 2000 and 2001, is indexed for inflation up to 2006, when it reaches $1 million (see Table 9.2, p.164).

enue Code Section 6166 extension or assets that would have to be sold at a sacrifice price.

Closely held business interest: up to 14 years if more than 35 percent of the adjusted gross estate consists of a closely held business.

If you fail to pay the tax when it is due, the estate will be subject to a penalty of 5 percent per month (to a maximum of 25 percent) unless you can show reasonable cause for the delay. And if you cannot pay the tax because all assets have been distributed to the beneficiaries, they will become personally liable for the tax in proportion to the assets distributed to them.

VALUATION OF THE GROSS ESTATE

Once you have listed all the items that comprise the gross estate, you must place a fair market value on them. Fair market value is defined as "the price at which the property would change hands between a willing buyer and a willing seller, neither being under compulsion to buy or sell and both having knowledge of the relevant facts."

This valuation is easy with respect to securities, because they generally have a market value that is published daily. The value of real estate can be established by examining selling prices and tax assessments of comparable properties, or by consulting an appraiser or a realtor. A solely owned business or a professional practice, however, presents a more difficult problem.

The fair market value of an interest in a sole proprietorship, a limited liability company, or a partnership is the net amount that a willing buyer would pay a willing seller when neither is under any compulsion and both have reasonable knowledge of the relevant facts, including:

> a fair appraisal of all the assets of the business;
> the demonstrated earning capacity of the business;
> other applicable factors used in the evaluation of corporate stock.

In calculating the tax, you can, as we have noted, choose to make the valuation of assets either as of the date of death or six months thereafter. Since the estate tax return is not due until nine months after death, you have the opportunity to use whichever figure reduces the tax obligation. Once the choice is made, however, it is irrevocable.

DEDUCTIONS

The most important deduction from the gross estate is known as the unlimited marital deduction, which, in many cases, reduces the estate's value sufficiently so that the estate avoids any estate tax. This deduction allows the surviving spouse to exempt from the estate tax all property that passes from the deceased to her, whether by bequest, by inheritance, by joint ownership, by revocable living trust, by pay-on-death and transfer-on-death accounts or as proceeds of life insurance. Although this deduction may exempt the estate from estate tax, it may create tax problems for the surviving spouse (and her survivors), since there will be no further marital deduction as to the inherited assets on her subsequent death, unless, of course, she remarries

Additional deductions from the gross estate include funeral expenses, administration expenses (executor, attorney, and accountant fees and court costs), paid claims against the estate, unpaid mortgages, uninsured losses incurred during estate settlement, and charitable bequests.

CREDITS AGAINST THE TAX

Once all allowable deductions have been subtracted from the gross estate, the result is the taxable estate, on which the "tentative" estate tax is computed on a sliding scale from 37 to 55 percent. Once this tentative tax has been calculated, certain tax credits are allowed that may eliminate or substantially reduce the estate tax. The most important of these is the "unified gift and estate tax credit"—a credit of $220,550[1] that is allowed to every taxpayer who is a U.S. citizen and that can be applied against the federal gift and estate tax (see table 9.2). Once this credit is applied, estates with a value of $675,000 or less in years 2000 and 2001 pay no federal estate tax.

In addition, a credit is allowed for any gift taxes previously paid on the deceased's lifetime gifts of $10,000 (or $20,000 with the consent of the donor's spouse) and for foreign death taxes.

CALCULATING THE ESTATE TAX

Calculating the estate tax requires several steps. They are described below and illustrated in Figure 9.1.

---

[1] The estate-tax credit amount, which is $220,550 fordeaths during 2000 and 2001, is indexed for inflation up to 2006, when it reaches $1 million (see Table 9.2, p.164).

TABLE 9.2
Federal Unified Gift and Estate Tax Credit

For Gifts Made and Estates of Persons Dying During the Year	Unified Credit Amount	Estate Tax Exemption Amount
1987–1997	$192,800	$600,000
1998	$202,050	$625,000
1999	$211,300	$650,000
2000	$220,550	$675,000
2001	$220,550	$675,000
2002	$229,800	$700,000
2003	$229,800	$700,000
2004	$287,300	$850,000
2005	$326,300	$950,000
2006 and thereafter	$345,800	$1,000,000

Source: Internal Revenue Code Section 2010.

The first step is to calculate the value of the gross estate by totaling the deceased's assets. For estate tax purposes, the gross estate includes

> solely owned cash, stocks, bonds, real estate, household furnishings, motor vehicles, jewelry, collectibles, and other assets;
>
> proceeds from the deceased's life insurance and annuity contracts (the latter valued according to tables published by the IRS);
>
> the deceased's retirement benefits, including IRA and Keogh accounts and employer-sponsored pension and savings plans;
>
> lifetime gifts made with strings attached. If, for example, the deceased gifted his house to his daughter but retained the right to occupy it during his lifetime, the IRS regards the house as belonging to the deceased for tax purposes;
>
> assets held in the deceased's revocable living trust;
>
> assets held in the deceased's bank, brokerage and other accounts which designate a pay-on-death or transfer-on-death beneficiary;
>
> the deceased's share of jointly held assets. Half of the value is included if the deceased owned assets with a spouse or if the joint owner is someone other than a spouse (a friend, for example) and they acquired the assets by gift or inheri-

Figure 9.1

FEDERAL ESTATE TAX WORKSHEET

1. Deceased's gross estate   _____
2. Claims, debts, and taxes   _____
3. Administration and funeral expense   _____
4. Adjusted gross estate (line 1 minus lines 2 and 3) _____
5. Marital deduction   _____
6. Charitable deduction   _____
7. Taxable gifts made after 1976   _____
8. Taxable estate (line 4 plus line 7 minus lines 5 and 6) _____
9. Federal estate tax before credits (find the amount on line 8 in column A of the table below and read across to column B) _____
10. Unified credit against gift and estate tax $220,550[1]
11. Federal estate tax less unified credit (subtract line 10 from line 9 or fill in the amount from column C) _____
12. Credit for state death taxes paid (column D) _____
13. Estimated federal estate tax (line 11 minus line 12) _____

tance. If the deceased purchased assets together with a joint owner, the portion contributed by the deceased is included in his gross estate;

if the deceased lived in a community property state (Arizona, California, Idaho, Louisiana, Nevada, New Mexico, Texas, Washington, or Wisconsin) one-half of all assets which either spouse acquired, with the exception of inheritances, is included in the deceased's gross estate.

Once you have entered the total on line 1 of Figure 9.1, your next step is to enter (on line 2) the deceased's outstanding debts: mortgage balances, unsecured loans, credit card balances, income taxes, and property taxes.

On line 3, enter the total of funeral and burial expenses and the expenses of settling the estate—that is, court costs, executor's fees

---

[1] The estate tax credit amount, which is $220,550 for years 2000 and 2001, is indexed for inflation up to 2006, when it reaches $345,800 (see Table 9.2, p.164).

and expenses, and payments to accountants, lawyers, real estate brokers, appraisers, and other persons employed by the state.

To determine the adjusted gross estate (line 4), subtract both lines 2 and 3 from line 1.

If there is a surviving spouse, determine the value of the assets left to him or her and enter it on line 5. (Obviously, if the entire estate was left to a surviving spouse, there will be no estate tax payable.) Then enter on line 6 the total of charitable bequests, and on line 7 enter the total of all charitable gifts made by the deceased during his lifetime since 1976. (To determine the value of these charitable gifts, check the federal gift tax return that the deceased should have filed after making them.)

The total estate consists of (line 7 + line 4) - (line 5 + line 6). You can now use Table 9.3 to estimate the estate's tentative tax before the unified tax credit is applied. From the amount shown in the left-hand column, you subtract $220,800 the "unified credit" for the years 2000 and 2001 which is allowed regardless of the size of the estate, and any gift tax that the deceased paid after 1986. Finally, subtract any credit allowed for state death taxes. This final figure, to be entered on line 13, is the federal estate tax.

TABLE 9.3
Federal Gift and Estate Tax Rates

Amount Subject to Tentative Tax ($)		Tax Rate on Excess over
Exceeding	but Not Exceeding	Tax on Amount in First Column	Amounts in ($)First Column[2] (%)
—	10,000	—	18
10,000	20,000	1,800	20
20,000	40,000	3,800	22
40,000	60,000	8,200	24
60,000	80,000	13,000	26
80,000	100,000	18,200	28
100,000	150,000	23,800	30
150,000	250,000	38,800	32
250,000	500,000	70,800	34
500,000	750,000	155,800	37
750,000	1,000,000	248,300	39
1,000,000	1,250,000	345,800	41

TABLE 9.3
Federal Gift and Estate Tax Rates *(continued)*

Amount Subject to Tentative Tax ($)		Tax on Amount in First Column	Tax Rate on Excess over Amounts in ($)First Column[2] (%)
Exceeding	but Not Exceeding		
1,250,000	1,500,000	448,300	43
1,500,000	2,000,000	555,800	45
2,000,000	2,500,000	780,800	49
2,500,000	3,000,000	1,025,800	53
3,000,000	—	1,290,800	55

[2] The tax above shall be increased by 5 percent of the amount by which the transfer exceeds $10,000,000 but does not exceed the amount at which the average tax rate is 55 percent.

Source: Internal Revenue Code Section 2001(c).

PAYING THE FEDERAL ESTATE TAX

Usually, you must pay the tax when the return is due—that is, within nine months of the death—and payment must be made even if you are granted an extension of time for filing the return. However, you may be granted an extension of time for payment of the tax if you can show why it is impractical or impossible for the estate to make full payment on the due date. The usual extension of time to pay is 12 months, but the IRS can extend the time for payment for as long as 10 years. And if a closely held business comprises 50 percent of the gross estate, you may be allowed to pay 50 percent of the tax in installments.

Whatever the difficulties you encounter, you must make certain that the tax is paid on time. If you neglect this payment, you can be subjected to substantial penalties and the IRS has the right to collect the tax from beneficiaries who have already received their shares of the estate.

STATE ESTATE AND INHERITANCE TAXES

If the deceased's state of residence imposes an inheritance tax (see Table 9.4) or an estate tax (see Table 9.5), you may need to file a state return. State law should be consulted to determine the filing requirements, the taxes due, and the responsibility for filing the return and paying the tax.

TABLE 9.4
State Inheritance Tax Rates and Exemptions
Selected Categories of Heirs As of December 31, 1997

	Rate			Exemptions ($ Thousands)			
State	Spouse, Child, or Parent	Brother or Sister	Other than Relative	Spouse	Child/ Parent	Brother or Sister	Other than Relative
Connecticut	2–8%	4–10%	8–14%	All	$50	$6	$1
Delaware	2–4	5–10	10–16	70	25	5	1
Indiana	1–10	7–15	10–20	All	100	0.5	0.1
Iowa	Exempt	5–10	10–15	All	All	None	None
Kansas	1–5	3–12.5	10–15	All	30	5	None
Kentucky	2–10	2–10	6–16	All	5(a) (b)	1 (a)	0.5
Louisiana (c)	2–3	5–7	5–10	All	25	1	0.5
Maryland	1	10	10	(d)	(d)	0.15	0.15
Montana	2–8	4–16	8–32	All	All/7	1	None
Nebraska	1	6–9	6–18	All	10	2	0.5
New Hampshire	Exempt	18	18	All	All	None	None
New Jersey	Exempt	11–16	15–16	All	All	0.5	0.5
North Carolina	1–12	4–16	8–17	All	33.15 credit	None	None

Pennsylvania	6	15	15	All	2	None	None
South Dakota	Exempt/3.75–7.5/3–15	4–20	6–30	All	30/3	0.5	0.1
Tennessee	5.5–9.5	5.5–9.5	5.5–9.5	600	600	600	600
Texas	(e)	(e)	(e)	(e)	(e)	(e)	(e)

(a) For all other, the exemption is the greater of the statutory amount or (1) one-fourth of each beneficiary's interest, if the decedent dies between July 1, 1995, and June 30, 1996; (2) one-half of each beneficiary's interest, if the decedent dies between July 1, 1996, and June 30, 1997; (3) three-fourths of each beneficiary's interest, if the decedent dies between July 1, 1997, and June 30, 1998; or (4) each beneficiary's total inheritable interest, if the decedent dies after June 30, 1998.

(b) Exemption is $20,000 for infant child or mentally disabled (natural or adopted).

(c) All tax rates will be reduced by 18% for all estates of persons dying after June 30, 1998, through June 30, 2001.

(d) No tax on transfers of real property and first $100,000 of property other than real property.

(e) The amount due is the portion of the federal credit attributable to property in Texas. Only estates that have federal estate tax liabilities are subject to the inheritance tax.

Note: In addition to an inheritance tax, all states listed also levy an estate tax, generally to assure full absorption of the federal credit.

Source: Commerce Clearing House and respective State Revenue Departments.

Most states impose either of two kinds of death tax: an inheritance tax, which is payable by each beneficiary receiving an inheritance; or an estate tax, which is payable by the estate itself.

A number of states currently levy a tax—variously called an inheritance, legacy, or succession tax—on the inheritance received by each beneficiary. This tax is payable to the state in which the deceased resided, regardless of the residence of the beneficiary.

Various exemptions are allowed, depending on the value of the inheritance and the relationship of the beneficiary to the deceased. Typically, the deceased's surviving spouse, children, and grandchildren are either partially or totally exempt. Other beneficiaries, often including siblings, must pay the full inheritance tax in those states that levy it.

Although inheritance taxes are payable by the beneficiaries, the deceased's will may specify that the tax is to be paid by the estate on their behalf. In any event, it is your responsibility as executor to make sure that the tax is paid, because the court will normally insist that you file a tax clearance certificate, issued by the state treasurer's office, before it will sign an order closing the estate and discharging you from your responsibilities.

A number of states impose an estate tax. Some impose this tax even on relatively small estates (for example, as low as $100,000), but the tax rate may approximate only 5 percent of the estate's value. Other states tax only those estates valued at more than the federal estate tax exclusion amount, $675,000 for the years 2000 and 2001. In some states that tax only large estates, the state tax is eliminated by the federal estate tax credit. Thus, an estate that is exempt from the federal estate tax will not be subject to the state estate tax. Table 9.5 presents both the tax rates and the exemptions.

TABLE 9.5

State Estate Tax Rates and Exemptions
(As of December 31, 1997)

State	Rate (On Net Estate After Exemptions) (b)	Maximum Rate Applies Above	Exemption
Alabama	Maximum Federal credit (c), (d)	$10,040,000	$60,000 (c)
Alaska	Maximum Federal credit (c), (d)	10,040,000	60,000 (c)
Arizona	Maximum Federal credit (c), (d)	10,040,000	60,000 (c)

TABLE 9.5
State Estate Tax Rates and Exemptions
(As of December 31, 1997) *(continued)*

State	Rate (On Net Estate After Exemptions) (b)	Maximum Rate Applies Above	Exemption
Arkansas	Maximum Federal credit (c), (d)	10,040,000	60,000 (c)
California	Maximum Federal credit (c), (d)	10,040,000	60,000 (c)
Colorado	Maximum Federal credit (c), (d)	10,040,000	60,000 (c)
Florida	Maximum Federal credit (c), (d)	10,040,000	60,000 (c)
Georgia	Maximum Federal credit (c), (d)	10,040,000	60,000 (c)
Hawaii	Maximum Federal credit (c), (d)	10,040,000	60,000 (c)
Idaho	Maximum Federal credit (c), (d)	10,040,000	60,000 (c)
Illinois	Maximum Federal credit (c), (d)	10,040,000	60,000 (c)
Maine	Maximum Federal credit (c), (d)	10,040,000	60,000 (c)
Massachusetts	Maximum Federal credit (c), (d)	10,040,000	60,000 (c)
Michigan	Maximum Federal credit (c), (d)	10,040,000	60,000 (c)
Minnesota	Maximum Federal credit (c), (d)	10,040,000	60,000 (c)
Mississippi	1% on first 60,000 to 16%	10,000,000	600,000
Missouri	Maximum Federal credit (c), (d)	10,040,000	60,000 (c)
Nevada	Maximum Federal credit (c), (d)	10,040,000	60,000 (c)
New Mexico	Maximum Federal credit (c), (d)	10,040,000	60,000 (c)
New York	2% on first 50,000 to 21%	10,100,000	Varies
North Dakota	Maximum Federal credit (c), (d)	10,040,000	60,000 (c)
Ohio	2% on first 40,000 to 7%	500,000	10,000 (e)
Oklahoma	0.5% on first 10,000 to 10% (f)	10,000,000	(g)
Oregon	Maximum Federal credit (c), (d)	10,040,000	60,000 (c)
Rhode Island	2% on first 25,000 to 9%	1,000,000	25,000 (h)
South Carolina	Maximum Federal credit (c), (d)	10,040,000	60,000 (c)
Utah	Maximum Federal credit (c), (d)	10,040,000	60,000 (c)
Vermont	Maximum Federal credit (c), (d)	10,040,000	60,000 (c)
Virginia	Maximum Federal credit (c), (d)	10,040,000	60,000 (c)
Washington	Maximum Federal credit (c), (d)	10,040,000	60,000 (c)
West Virginia	Maximum Federal credit (c), (d)	10,040,000	60,000 (c)
Wisconsin	Maximum Federal credit (c), (d)	10,040,000	60,000 (c)
Wyoming	Maximum Federal credit (c), (d)	10,040,000	60,000 (c)

TABLE 9.5

State Estate Tax Rates and Exemptions

As of December 31, 1997 *(continued)*

State	Rate (On Net Estate After Exemptions) (b)	Maximum Rate Applies Above	Exemption
District of Columbia	Maximum Federal credit (c), (d)	10,040,000	60,000 (c)

(a) Excludes states shown in inheritance tax table (9.4) which levy an estate tax in addition to their inheritance taxes to insure full absorption of the federal credit.

(b) The rates generally are in addition to graduated absolute amounts.

(c) Maximum federal credit allowed under the 1954 Code for state estate taxes paid is expressed as a percentage of the taxable estate (after $60,000 exemption) in excess of $40,000, plus a graduated absolute amount. The $60,000 exemption is allowed under the state death tax credit.

(d) A tax on nonresident estates is imposed on the proportionate share of the estate which the property located in the state bears to the entire estate wherever situated.

(e) A credit equal to the lesser of $500 or the amount of the estate is allowed. A marital deduction is allowed in an amount equal to the net value of any asset passing from the decedent to the receiving spouse. But only to the extent that the asset is included in the value of the Ohio gross estate. Property passing to surviving spouse is entirely excluded.

(f) Rates apply only to lineal heirs, for collateral heirs the rates vary from 1% on the first $10,000 to 15% on amounts of $1,000,000 or more.

(g) Exemption is a total aggregate of $175,000 for father, mother, child, and named relatives. Property passing to surviving spouse is entirely excluded.

(h) Marital deduction is $175,000.

Source: Commerce Clearing House.

≈ **10** ≈

MANAGING, DISTRIBUTING, AND CLOSING THE PROBATE ESTATE

As we have noted, one of your first tasks as executor is to locate, collect, and assemble all of the deceased's probate assets, which then become your responsibility. If the probate process is swift and efficient, this responsibility should be short-lived, since you will quickly distribute the estate's assets to the will-designated beneficiaries or if there is no will, to the heirs at law. All too often, however, probate administration drags on for many months. In the meantime you will remain responsible for managing the assets—that is, protecting their value, collecting whatever income they produce, and paying whatever obligations they incur, including state and federal taxes on their income.

MANAGING THE ESTATE

To begin the management process, you should evaluate each of the estate's assets and attempt to determine whether it is productive and likely to maintain its current value. Nonproductive assets or "wasting" assets—those that lose value with the passage of time— should be earmarked for immediate liquidation and should be sold at the highest possible price to prevent further devaluation. Motor vehicles and boats, for example, or business equipment not being used in a continuing enterprise, require continued maintenance and insurance, and may quickly lose their value through obsolescence and depreciation. Similarly, agricultural produce and livestock must be sold immediately if they are to yield the best price.

Generally, nonproductive or wasting assets can be sold without obtaining a court order; but if these assets have been specifically bequeathed by the deceased's will, you should first obtain a court order or the written consent of all interested persons.

Although managing the estate's assets—especially if they are substantial or complex—may strike you as a heavy responsibility, there are two points that you should bear in mind. First, you are expected to act not as a financial expert but as a "prudent person." This means that you are under no obligation to attempt to forecast a market—whether for securities, real estate, or an ongoing business—and that you are not obligated to maximize yield on the assets. You need only act prudently to see that the assets do not depreciate through your failure to exercise reasonable care.

Second, you are entitled to pay with estate funds any needed professionals—lawyers, accountants, financial advisers—that you may choose to hire to assist you in making decisions that are within the limits of your powers established by the will, by the court, and by state law.

REAL PROPERTY

Because you are required to maintain the estate's real property— that is, a home, a vacation cottage or condominium, rental property, or vacant land—you are entitled to use estate funds to repair (but not to improve) it. In addition, you must pay, from estate funds, all mortgage payments, insurance premiums, real estate taxes, utility bills, and maintenance costs that become due on the property in order to prevent foreclosure, deterioration, or loss by casualty. You must make certain, moreover, that the insurance coverage is adequate, since you can be held personally liable should a loss occur that exceeds the coverage that a reasonably prudent person would maintain on the property.

PERSONAL PROPERTY

In some cases, the cost of storing, maintaining, and insuring personal property—such as boats and vehicles—may exceed the value of the property itself. You should therefore avoid this situation by taking one of the following courses of action. If the estate has sufficient assets to meet its obligations (creditors' claims, taxes, and the expenses of administration), you may petition the court for an order to make an early distribution of the property to the entitled beneficiary. On the other hand, if the estate does not have sufficient assets, you may petition the court for an order to sell the property immediately. In either event, a court order will protect you from personal liability resulting from disposal of the property.

INVESTMENT OF ESTATE FUNDS

Because you are required to pay the estate's creditors as well as taxes, court costs, and administration expenses, it is important that you carefully estimate these obligations and make sure that you retain sufficient estate funds to pay them. Because the payment of such obligations is not likely to be immediate, the funds should, in the interim, be kept in a form that yields the highest possible return. But they can be invested only in instruments authorized by the will, the orders of the court, and the laws of the state.

Generally speaking, state law limits the investment of estate funds to federally insured interest-bearing accounts, short-term U.S. government obligations, readily marketable secured loan arrangements and similar investments that carry minimal risk, or other investments that a prudent person would regard as reasonable.

Investment of estate funds in stocks, bonds, or mutual funds, if authorized by the will, must be made with great care because, what with the payment of brokerage commissions, mutual-fund loads, and early-redemption fees, a favorable return often requires a time span longer than the duration of the typical probate administration. In general, investments in out-of-state securities, with the exception of state or municipal bonds, are unwise, because they may be difficult to control or sell. But if the estate's assets already include such investments, there is no requirement that they be sold immediately. Of course, if you can obtain the written consent of the beneficiaries or a court order, your menu of investment choices can be broadened considerably.

USING INVESTMENT COUNSELORS

If the estate's assets include stocks or bonds, no liability will accrue to you if you sell them immediately instead of holding them in the hope that their prices will rise. You may, however, obtain expert advice from an investment counselor on the advisability of retaining or selling them, and the cost of such advice is payable with estate funds. Although in most states the fiduciary responsibility to the estate remains yours, some states permit responsibility for the handling of investments to be shifted to an investment counselor.

Before deciding to use an investment counselor, however, you may want to bear in mind that the accreditation of investment counselors is extremely weak in some states, that their overall performance record has not been distinguished, and that those counselors who are affiliated with brokerage firms, mutual funds, or insurance companies have often been accused of providing advice that yields them commissions rather than benefiting their clients.

A GOING BUSINESS

If the estate's assets include an interest in a business—a sole proprietorship, a limited liability company, a partnership, or a closely held corporation—you should look first for guidance in the will, the partnership agreement, or the corporate shareholders' agreement, since these may contain specific provisions governing its disposal. If the will specifies that the business shall or may continue, you will not be held responsible for any consequent business losses in the absence of bad faith or lack of diligence in its management. If the will contains no provision about continuance, you are authorized to continue it for only a short period of time following the issuance of your letters of authority. This short "winding-up" period is intended to give you time to close, evaluate, and liquidate the business with adequate return to the estate. If circumstances call for a longer period, a court order is often required.

If you plan to continue the operation of a business, you should consult IRS Publication 334, *Tax Guide for Small Business*, which explains the tax and employment laws with which you will have to comply.

SOLE PROPRIETORSHIPS AND LIMITED LIABILITY COMPANIES

If the will does not specify that a sole proprietorship or a limited liability company is to be liquidated, the survivors may indicate a willingness to continue it. As executor, you must determine whether such an arrangement is in the best interest of the estate. A petition to the court to permit continuation of the business may be necessary if the will is silent on the issue. If, however, funds from the sale of the business are needed to pay creditors, taxes, or administration expenses, you may be required to sell the business in order to meet these obligations.

PARTNERSHIPS

If the deceased was involved in a partnership, the partnership agreement may specify the course of action to be taken on the death of one of the partners—dissolution of the partnership, purchase of the deceased's interest, for example, or continuation of the partnership with the deceased's survivors retaining an interest. Such an agreement is binding on you and on the estate. If there is no such provision, the surviving partner(s) are obliged to wind up the partnership, settle its affairs without delay, and provide you with a detailed accounting along with payment for the deceased's interest in the business, including any undistributed profits.

CLOSELY HELD CORPORATIONS

If the estate's assets include stock in a closely held corporation, your management of the deceased's shares may depend on several factors. If the deceased was not the sole stockholder there may exist a shareholder's agreement that addresses and governs the disposition of the deceased's shares. The shares may, for example, have to be offered first to the surviving shareholders or to the corporation at a price or formula specified in the agreement. Or there may be a life insurance policy specifically purchased for the funding of a buyout of the estate in the event of a shareholder's death.

If the will bequeaths the stock to designated beneficiaries, you must obtain their consent before taking any action to dispose of it. And if the estate consists of stock in a professional corporation (sometimes known as a P.C.), state law may prohibit such stock from being held by anyone who is not a member of that profession. This prohibition may force a dissolution of the corporation.

If the stock cannot be sold because there is simply no market for it, you should consider taking action to terminate the business, sell the corporate assets, and dissolve the corporation. Usually, the corporation's bylaws or shareholders' agreement set forth the procedure that must be followed for dissolution. If not, your course of action will be governed by your state's corporation laws.

DISTRIBUTING THE ASSETS

Once you have paid from the estate's assets all the probate admin-istration expenses, all taxes, and all claims allowed against the estate, you are ready to distribute the remaining assets to the bene-ficiaries designated in the will, or to the heirs at law if there was no will (see Chapter 11) and close the estate. Before doing so, however, you are required by some states to file an accounting with the court, and to apply for approval of your plan for distribution and for your discharge as the executor.

In some states, this petition must be filed with the court and served on all interested persons within a specified time. Florida law, for example, requires the petition to be filed within 12 months of the issuance of your letters of authority if no federal estate tax is due, or 12 months from the date on which the federal estate tax is due.

If no objection to your accounting and petition is filed within a specified time—usually 30 days—you may then distribute the estate's remaining assets according to your proposed plan without a court order. If, however, there are objections, the court will approve or modify your proposed distribution and then sign an order dis-charging you on condition that you distribute the estate as ordered. Once you have made the distribution, you must file proof of distri-bution, typically in the form of receipts signed by the recipients (see Figure 10.1, p. 186). At this point you are formally discharged and the estate is closed.

Distribution, however, is not always a straightforward proce-dure—for a number of reasons. To begin with, there may not be suf-ficient probate assets left to satisfy all bequests specified in the will. For example, advancements made to beneficiaries by the deceased before death, and state laws on spousal rights, homestead rights, and family allowances, may reduce or deplete the estate's assets and thus prevent you from carrying out all of the will's bequests to the letter. On the other hand, some beneficiaries may disclaim their bequest, since no one can be forced to accept an inheritance (see p. 183). Hence, before you proceed with any distribution of assets to the beneficiaries, each of these issues needs careful consideration.

In such circumstances, convening a meeting with all the benefi-ciaries—or perhaps only with those primarily affected—can do much to clarify the issues and prevent misunderstanding, disappointment, or hostility among them. You must bear in mind, however, that you, as the executor, have the final say, subject to the terms of the will, any court-ordered modification, and the laws of the state.

ISSUES AFFECTING THE WILL

BENEFICIARY SURVIVAL AND LAPSE

At common law, if a beneficiary should die between the execution of the will and the death of the testator, the bequest to that beneficiary lapses—that is, the gift becomes void—and the bequeathed property is distributed according to the will's residuary "catchall" clause. If the will contained no residuary clause specifying disposition of "the rest, residue, and remainder," of the estate and named no contingent beneficiary, the property is distributed according to the state's intestacy law.

To avoid this situation, most states have passed "anti-lapse" laws, which permit the descendants of certain classes of predeceased beneficiaries to stand in their ancestor's place for purposes of receiving the bequest. Under Michigan's anti-lapse law, for example, if a predeceasing beneficiary was a member of the testator's immediate family, the bequest does not lapse, but passes to that beneficiary's children or grandchildren.

Although one must survive the deceased in order to inherit from him, common law does not specify the length of time of survival, but the will may, in fact specify it. Absent any specification in the will, however, any measurable length of time, such as one minute—or, theoretically, one second—is sufficient. Hence, when the survival of an heir affects the inheritances of other heirs, the timing of the death may become a hotly contested issue.

In an attempt to resolve the problem, many states have adopted the Uniform Simultaneous Death Act, which specifies that "when there is no sufficient evidence that persons have died otherwise than simultaneously, the property of each person shall be disposed of as if he had survived." The act does not, however, solve the problem completely, because it implies that if there *is* adequate proof of the sequence of deaths, the surviving heir, no matter how brief the time of survival, will be entitled to his share of the deceased's estate.

A provision in the Uniform Probate Code eliminates this problem in most situations. Drawing on a frequently used estate-planning device, the code requires that in order to qualify as a beneficiary a person must survive the deceased by at least 120 days. This provision substantially reduces litigation about who has survived.

ADEMPTION: WHEN A BEQUEATHED ASSET IS NO LONGER IN THE ESTATE

Occasionally a bequest fails because the asset bequeathed is no longer in the estate of the deceased—because, during his lifetime, the deceased used up, sold, or gave away the asset either to someone else or to the intended beneficiary. In general, if the item is no longer in the deceased's probate estate because it was sold or given away to someone else, the beneficiary gets nothing—a result known as ademption by extinction. If, on the other hand, the deceased, during his lifetime, gave the item to the designated beneficiary with the specific intent of reducing his or her inheritance, this is known as ademption by satisfaction. That is, the item is counted as an "advance" toward the beneficiary's bequest and is intended to prevent the beneficiary from claiming a disproportionate share of the estate.

Generally it is difficult to determine whether a gift made during the lifetime of the deceased was intended as an outright gift unrelated to any bequest or a gift representing an "advance" on a bequest. To resolve this question, the Uniform Probate Code specifies that if a lifetime gift is to be construed as an advancement, there must be written evidence stating that the testator intended—or the beneficiary accepted—the gift as an "advance" on a bequest.

ABATEMENT

The executor may discover that—perhaps as a result of creditors' claims, taxes, expenses of administration, a general insufficiency of funds, or an election by the spouse (see below)—there are not enough probate assets to satisfy all bequests in the will. When this occurs, bequests must be diminished by a process known as abatement.

At common law, and under the Uniform Probate Code, in the absence of provisions in the will to the contrary, the order of abatement is determined by a rank order of priority. The first assets to be abated are "intestate" assets—that is, assets in the probate estate that have not been distributed by the will (for example, a lapsed bequest). Beyond intestate assets, the next abatement involves assets covered by the residuary clause. If these abatements do not make up the shortage, "general" legacies—"I give to my nephew, John Smith, $10,000"—are abated. Lastly, specific legacies—"I give my $10,000 diamond ring to my daughter Jane"—may be abated.

SPOUSAL RIGHTS

Regardless of what the will leaves to a spouse, the laws of the state may supersede the will. Most states give the surviving spouse either a right to "take against" the deceased's will or some elective rights to the deceased's property. This right is variously called the elective share, the forced share, or the statutory share. The term we shall use in the following discussion is the *elective* share.

Upon the death of a spouse, the surviving spouse is required by law to decide, usually within 30 days following notification from the executor, whether to take the bequests, if any, provided in the will or to take the spouse's elective share. This elective share may, in fact, be greater or less than the amount bequeathed in the will.

No one can dictate this choice to the spouse unless the spouse is incompetent, in which case the spouse's guardian makes it. However, you, as the executor, have the responsibility of giving the spouse notice of this right and full opportunity to make the election within the specified time limit. This election not only determines what the spouse will get but also affects the assets remaining for other beneficiaries. If no election is made within the time limit, the spouse forfeits the elective share and takes whatever bequests are specified in the will.

In some states, the spouse's elective share is equal to one-third of the value of the probate estate. Hence, if the deceased's will bequeaths to the spouse an amount equal to the spouse's elective share, that is the most that she can receive, and the other beneficiaries will receive the balance of the estate's assets.

Whether the spouse's elective share is greater or less than the willed bequest, the spouse's decision about which to elect depends on a number of factors. Even if the spouse's elective share is greater than what the will provides, the spouse may reject it if her own estate is ample, or if the elective share would increase her tax liability or that of *her* estate on her death. Indeed, she may, if she prefers, disclaim the willed bequest entirely (see p. 183) so as to increase the share of the estate's assets available for distribution to other beneficiaries.

In most states, a spouse's decision to take the elective share applies only to probate assets. Regardless of the spousal election, the deceased's jointly held assets would pass to the surviving joint owner and life insurance proceeds would pass to the policy's designated beneficiary, and neither would be counted as assets subject to the spouse's elective share. In a few states, however—particularly those that have adopted the Uniform Probate Code—the value of certain nonprobate assets, referred to as the "augmented estate," is counted in calculating the value of the spouse's elective share. Under the Uniform Probate Code, this augmented estate consists of the value of property transferred by the deceased to the spouse during marriage, including assets jointly owned or held in a revocable living trust. The value of this augmented estate will be credited against and thus reduce the surviving spouse's elective share.

HOMESTEAD RIGHTS AND FAMILY ALLOWANCES

Because the probate process may continue for many months before the estate can be settled, distributed, and closed, all states provide some protection against financial hardship for the surviving spouse and, in some cases, for the deceased's minor children. These protective laws include a "homestead right," which usually permits the spouse and minor children to occupy the deceased's home for a specified period of time, even though the home may have been bequeathed to someone else. In some states the surviving spouse has the right to reside there for the rest of her life, whether or not the deceased left minor children.

In addition to the homestead right, the spouse has the right, in all states, to apply for and receive a court-ordered allowance from the probate estate for the support of herself and her minor children. This "family allowance" takes priority over all other debts of the estate, and it is payable even if it renders the estate insolvent. Moreover, it is available to the spouse in addition to what she may receive as a beneficiary named in the will, or if she chooses to take the elective share, or if she asserts her homestead rights.

Because it enjoys priority, the family allowance can, if the court makes it large enough, reduce or even eliminate other bequests. If the estate is small, it could be entirely depleted by the family allowance, in which case there would be no remaining estate assets to administer, even though creditors' claims go unpaid and the will's bequests are totally preempted.

The amount and duration of the family allowance is determined by the court, which takes into consideration the size of the estate and the spouse's age, health, and standard of living. It is these considerations that often give rise to disputes because the executor, the spouse, the other affected beneficiaries, and the court may arrive at quite different figures. But, although it may hear arguments and admit evidence from the competing parties, the court has the final say.

The court has no discretion, however, as to who is to receive the family allowance. On the one hand, a spouse who has been separated (but not divorced) from the deceased for many years may nevertheless be entitled to the allowance. On the other hand, a surviving widow, no matter how needy, will lose her right to the allowance immediately upon her remarriage.

Court-ordered payment of the family allowance is not automatic. It must be applied for by the surviving spouse within a reasonable time after the death. If the spouse is in serious financial need—and especially if she is not the sole beneficiary named in the will or if several creditors have viable claims against the estate—the spouse should be sure that the petition for family allowance is filed promptly with the court. On the other hand, if the spouse already has adequate funds (from her own or from jointly held assets, for example, or from life insurance proceeds) and is also the sole beneficiary of the estate, she may prefer to forgo the allowance, use her own funds for support, and simply wait for the probate estate to be settled and closed, thus avoiding the expense and delay of a petition and hearing on the issue.

DISCLAIMING AN INHERITANCE

Because a bequest need not be accepted, any beneficiary has the right to disclaim it. If, for example, the will leaves $100,000 "to my brother, Robert Smith, if he survives me, otherwise to Robert's daughter, Jennifer" and if Robert disclaims the bequest, he is deemed to have predeceased the testator, and thus his daughter, Jennifer, the contingent beneficiary named in the will, receives the $100,000.

There are several reasons why a beneficiary may disclaim a bequest, among them the possibility that another survivor has a greater need for the bequest. If, for example, Robert is wealthy or elderly, his eventual estate may be subject to a substantial federal estate tax (see Chapter 9). By disclaiming the bequest, he diverts the $100,000 inheritance to his daughter without its ever being included in his own taxable estate.

On the other hand, Robert may be beset by numerous creditors who will seek to claim the $100,000 bequest as soon as he receives it. By disclaiming it, he places the money beyond the reach of his creditors, since they have no legal basis for making claims against an inheritance that passes to his daughter.

If the will does not name a contingent beneficiary, then Robert's disclaimed bequest passes to the "residuary beneficiaries"—that is, those to whom the will bequeaths "all the rest, residue, and remainder" of the estate. If they also disclaim it, then any surviving heirs at law who have not been named in the will receive it in order of priority according to state intestacy laws. If the first entitled heir at law also disclaims it, it passes to the next entitled heir, and so on. In some states, if the will fails to name a contingent beneficiary, a disclaimed inheritance may pass to those persons named in existing anti-lapse statutes.

Any beneficiary considering a disclaimer must comply strictly with the state-imposed time limit for making disclaimers, and should confirm the identity of the substitute beneficiary and his or her willingness to accept the disclaimed bequest. In addition, the disclaiming beneficiary must give written notice of the disclaimer promptly so that the distribution of assets can be revised accordingly. For federal estate tax purposes, the disclaimer must be in writing, signed before acceptance of the inheritance, and delivered to the executor within nine months after the deceased's death.

THE MECHANICS OF DISTRIBUTION

As we have seen, any of the factors we have discussed can materially change the bequests specified in the will. Hence, if you have not already done so, you may, at this point, want to convene the likely beneficiaries for a meeting to explain any changes that must be made in the bequests or the proposed distribution.

In many cases the probate estate may be divided readily into fractional shares and distributed in kind to the beneficiaries. In other cases the beneficiaries may agree to a liquidation of the estate's assets and a distribution of the cash proceeds. It is a common misconception that all assets must be sold during probate administration, but this is not the case. On the contrary, distribution of the estate's assets in kind is usually intended by the testator and is generally favored by state law.

REAL ESTATE AND PERSONAL PROPERTY

Distribution of real estate may be accomplished by delivering a court "order assigning residue" that describes the real estate and specifies the beneficiary. To distribute untitled personal property—jewelry, antiques, or a clock collection, for example—you will likewise obtain an order assigning residue and deliver it to the beneficiary. When the inheritance consists of titled personal property—a car for example— you complete and sign the transferor's portion of the certificate of title and deliver it to the beneficiary, along with copies of the death certificate and your letters of authority.

SECURITIES

Transfer and distribution of the estate's securities may be subject to the state-specified transfer requirements of the state of incorporation. Generally speaking, delivering to a broker the stock certificates, along with copies of the death certificate, your letters of authority, and a stock power with your signature guaranteed, is sufficient to get the stock reissued in the name of the entitled beneficiary.

U.S savings bonds held in the sole name of the deceased can be redeemed only by you as executor. They may be reissued, however, to the entitled beneficiary. A request for reissue should be made on Treasury Form PD1455, accompanied by copies of the death certificate and your letters of authority.

DISTRIBUTION TO MINORS

If a bequest to a minor, whether in property or in cash, does not exceed a specified amount—often $5,000—it can be delivered to the child's natural guardian—that is, the surviving parent—or to a court-appointed guardian if the guardian signs a written consent. If the guardian's consent cannot be obtained, or if the value of the bequest exceeds the state-specified maximum, distribution can be made only to a trustee for the minor (if a trust exists and is designated as the beneficiary) or to a court-appointed conservator of the minor's property. If the will specifies it, the distribution can

Figure 10.1

BENEFICIARY'S RECEIPT FOR
DISTRIBUTIVE SHARE

STATE OF MICHIGAN PROBATE COURT COUNTY OF	RECEIPT OF DISTRIBUTIVE SHARE	FILE NO.

Estate of _____

_____

THIS IS TO ACKNOWLEDGE that I have received of _____

_____ , Personal Representative of the estate, my

full share of personal property.

_____   _____

Date   Signature

also be made to the custodian of a custodial account for the child (see p. 42).

CASH DISTRIBUTIONS

Monetary distributions to beneficiaries should never be made in cash. Instead, the deceased's cash should be deposited in the estate's checking account so that checks can be written and delivered to the entitled beneficiaries. On the back of each check you might stamp or type words to the effect that any endorsement acknowledges complete distribution of the beneficiary's share of the estate. In the absence of receipts, these canceled checks, when filed with the court, constitute sufficient proof of receipt of payment.

OBTAINING RECEIPTS

Before you can be discharged as executor, you must satisfy the court that the estate's entitled beneficiaries have received their rightful shares. The best evidence of this consists of written receipts (see Figure 10.1) from each of the beneficiaries to whom you distribute assets.

In some states the receipt must not only describe the asset being distributed but also recite the authority pursuant to which the distribution is being made (for example, "pursuant to Article III of the will of Robert Smith"). In addition, if the distribution is the full and final share due to the person receiving it, the receipt should state this.

Once they have received their bequests, beneficiaries tend to lose interest in the probate administration process and hence may not bother to sign and return requested receipts. With respect to monetary bequests, the canceled check can serve as proof of payment. When personal property other than money is involved, it may be wise to withhold distribution until you have first received a signed receipt from the beneficiary.

CLOSING THE ESTATE

Once you have distributed the remaining assets to the beneficiaries, you are authorized to close the probate estate and thereby end your responsibilities as executor. To do this you must submit to the court a final accounting of all assets collected, all assets disbursed and distributed, and the balance, if any, remaining on hand to be distributed (see Figure 10.2).

State laws vary as to the steps required of you in winding up probate administration and closing the estate, but the procedures specified by the Uniform Probate Code are representative of the closing procedures required by many states.

Under the Uniform Probate Code, two different closing procedures are available. An *informal* procedure (sometimes called "closing by sworn statement") can be used if you feel that court approval of your settlement of the estate is unnecessary. A *formal* closing procedure (sometimes called "closing by court petition") is used if you want a formal court order settling and closing the estate and discharging you as the executor.

INFORMAL CLOSING

Under the code's informal closing procedure, you as the executor are not required to obtain an order from the court. You need merely file a sworn statement with the court no earlier than six months after your original appointment as executor. This sworn statement must recite that (1) notice to creditors has been published, (2) the deceased's probate estate has been fully distributed, (3) a copy of the sworn statement has been sent to all beneficiaries and to all creditors who remain unpaid, and (4) a written accounting of your

Figure 10.2

STATE OF MICHIGAN PROBATE COURT COUNTY OF CIRCUIT COURT - FAMILY DIVISION	ACCOUNT OF FIDUCIARY ☐ _____ Annual ☐ Final ☐ Interim *Number*	FILE NO.

Estate of _____

1. I, _____, am the _____
                Name   *Title*

of the estate and submit the following as my account, which covers the period
from _____ to _____ .
               Date   *Date*

This account contains a correct statement of all income and disbursements which have come to my knowledge.

2. **SUMMARY**

    Balance on hand from last account (or value of inventory
      if first account) .... $ _____

    Add income in this accounting period (total from
      Schedule A) .... $ _____

      Total assets accounted for....................................... $ _____

    Subtract disbursements in this accounting period
      (total from Schedule B) .... $ _____

    Total balance of assets remaining
      (itemize and describe in Schedule D).............................. $ _____

If additional sheets are required for Schedules A or B, place all itemization on those sheets and include only category totals on these schedules.

SCHEDULE A: Income in this accounting period		SCHEDULE B: Expenses and other disbursements, including distributions to devisees and beneficiaries	
Net gain, if any, from Schedule C		Net loss, if any, from Schedule C	
Total Income		**Total Expenses and Disbursements**	

Do not write below this line - For court use only

Figure 10.2 *(continued)*

SCHEDULE C: Gains and losses on disposition of assets (use only if needed)					
DESCRIPTION	DATE ACQUIRED	DATE SOLD	VALUE AT TIME ACQUIRED BY FIDUCIARY	NET SALES PRICE	GAIN (LOSS)

TOTAL GAIN (LOSS)
If gain, transfer to Schedule A;
if loss, transfer to Schedule B.

SCHEDULE D: Itemized assets remaining at end of accounting period	
If additional sheets are required, indicate on Schedule "See attached sheets".	

BALANCE OF ASSETS REMAINING (show this amount on summary)

3. The interested persons, addresses, and their representatives are identical to those appearing on the initial application/petition, except as follows:

4. This account lists all income and other receipts and expenses and other disbursements which have come to my knowledge.

5. ❑ a. No Michigan estate tax or inheritance tax is due.
 ❑ b. Michigan estate tax or inheritance tax
  ❑ is due.
  ❑ has been paid in full. (evidence of full payment from Michigan
   Department of Treasury is attached)

6. ❑ This account is not being filed with the court.

7. ❑ My fiduciary fees for this accounting period are $ _____.
Attached is a written description of the services performed.

Figure 10.2 *(continued)*

8. ❑ Attorney fees for this accounting period are $ _____. Attached is a written description of the services performed.

I declare under the penalties of perjury that this account has been examined by me and that its contents are true to the best of my information, knowledge, and belief.

_____
Date

_____   _____
Attorney signature   *Fiduciary signature*

_____   _____
Attorney name (type or print)   *Fiduciary name (type or print)*

_____   _____
Address   Bar no.   *Address*

_____   _____
City, state, zip   *Tel. no.*   *City, state, zip*   *Tel. no.*

For accounts that must be filed with the court.

NOTICE TO INTERESTED PERSONS

1. You must bring to the court's attention any objection you have to this account. The court will not review the account otherwise.
2. You have the right to review proofs of income and disbursements at a time reasonably convenient to the fiduciary and yourself.
3. You may object to all or part of an accounting by filing a written objection with the court before the court allows the account. You must pay a $15.00 filing fee to the court when you file the objection.
4. If an objection is filed and is not otherwise resolved, the court will conduct a hearing on the objection.

administration has been sent to all beneficiaries. In addition, if any allowed claims remain undischarged, your sworn statement must include an explanation of how they will be resolved.

After the passage of a state-specified period of time, your filing of the sworn statement has the effect of concluding probate administration of the estate and discharging you from further responsibilities. Your discharge takes effect one year after your filing of the statement, provided, however, that no beneficiaries or creditors have instituted proceedings against you for breach of your fiduciary duties within six months of your filing of the statement.

FORMAL CLOSING

Under the code's formal closing procedure, you, as the executor, may petition the court for an order of complete settlement of the estate, but your petition may not be considered by the court until the time for filing creditors' claims against the estate has expired.

Notice of your petition for formal closure must be given to all interested persons—beneficiaries, creditors, and heirs at laws. After conducting a hearing on the petition, the court has the power to issue orders on a broad range of matters, among them a determination of the persons entitled to distribution, approval of settlement, approval of your distribution of the assets, approval of your fees and expenses, discharge of you as the executor, and formal closing of the estate.

DISCHARGE OF THE EXECUTOR

If you have been discharged under a formal closing procedure (see Figure 10.3) or if your appointment has automatically terminated because one year has elapsed since you filed an informal closing statement, you have no authority to deal with any probate assets of the deceased that may be subsequently discovered and that may require probate administration. In order to transfer ownership of and settle such assets, survivors must seek and obtain a court order appointing a successor executor and reopening the deceased's probate estate. The original executor may be reappointed if, of course, he again agrees to serve.

Figure 10.3

STATE OF MICHIGAN PROBATE COURT COUNTY OF CIRCUIT COURT - FAMILY DIVISION	ORDER OF DISCHARGE	FILE NO.

In the matter of _____

1. Date of hearing: _____ Judge: _____
Bar no.

2. It appears the fiduciary in this matter has fully performed the duties required by law.

IT IS ORDERED:

3. _____ , _____ is discharged
       Name   *Title*

   and bond, if any, cancelled.

4. The matter/estate ❏ is closed.
                   ❏ is closed.

_____   _____
      Date   *Judge*

_____
Attorney name (type or print)   *Bar. no.*

_____
Address

_____
City, state, zip   *Tel. no.*

Part IV
SPECIAL SITUATIONS

≈ 11 ≈
WHEN THERE IS NO WILL

Although the estates of most people who die without having prepared a will are probably too small to require full probate administration, a significant number of people with substantial assets leave
no will, or leave a will that, for one reason or another, is declared
invalid by the probate court. In either situation, these people are
regarded as having died intestate.

In cases of intestacy, state law in effect imposes a will substitute
that specifies how the probate estate is to be administered and who
is entitled to receive an inheritance. In some cases the state-
imposed will essentially reflects what the deceased would have preferred had he signed a valid will, but in many cases it does not.

State intestacy laws cover the following issues, all of which are
usually specified in a will had the deceased left one:

- the identity of those persons entitled to inherit the deceased's
  probate assets—persons referred to as "heirs at law";
- a priority listing of persons entitled to appointment by the
  court as *administrator*—an office that carries the same responsibility as that of the executor or personal representative
  named in a will;
- the powers granted to the administrator and the circumstances under which he must be bonded;
- a priority listing of persons entitled to appointment by the
  court as guardians for the deceased's orphaned minor children.

APPOINTMENT OF THE ADMINISTRATOR

As Table 11.1 indicates, the deceased's close relatives usually have the highest priority for court appointment as the administrator. If a person with the highest priority declines to serve, the person at the next level of priority is offered the appointment. If no member of the family is willing to serve, sometimes a creditor, eager to have his claim paid from the estate's assets, may petition the court for appointment. The petition may be granted only after the heirs at law are notified.

TABLE 11.1
**Typical Priority Order for Appointment
As Administrator**

Priority Rank	Description of Candidates
1	Surviving spouse (or spouse's nominee)
2	Other heirs at law by degree of kinship (or their nominee)
3	Any creditor of the deceased

Once appointed, the administrator has essentially the same probate administration duties and responsibilities as the executor of a testate estate. These have been described in Chapter 7 through 10.

THE HEIRS AT LAW

The Uniform Probate Code (adopted by 16 states) dictates the distribution of the intestate estate's probate assets by dividing the deceased's relatives into distinct classes and establishing a priority sequence within each class. The classes consist of (1) a surviving spouse, (2) the deceased's children and grandchildren, (3) the deceased's parents, (4) the deceased's parents' children, (5) the deceased's grandparents, and (6) the deceased's grandparents' children (see Table 11.2). If none of these classes has a qualified member within it at the time of death, the code specifies that the estate goes to the state treasury, a result referred to as escheat. Intestacy laws make no provision for unmarried cohabitants.

In reality, this division into classes is often academic, because the code's distribution plan is rather generous to a surviving spouse. The suggested minimum for the spouse's share where there are surviving children—$150,000—is likely to exhaust the estate's probate assets. In addition to this $150,000, there is a family protection allowance of up to $25,000 payable from probate assets. These amounts are in addition to any assets the spouse might acquire from the deceased through joint ownership, pay-on-death and transfer-on-death accounts, retirement accounts, life insurance, or a living trust.

TABLE 11.2
Intestate Succession Under the Uniform Probate Code

If Deceased Is Survived[1] by	Deceased's Probate Estate Distributed as Follows
I (a) Spouse and descendants[2] (Born to deceased and spouse)	a) Spouse takes 1st $150,000 plus half of balance[5] b) Descendants share half of balance
I (b) Spouse and descendants[2] (Born to deceased alone)	a) Spouse takes 1st $100,000 plus half of balance[5] b) Issue share half of balance
II Spouse and Parents (No descendants)	a) Spouse takes 1st $200,000 plus three-fourths of balance b) Parents share half of balance
III Spouse only (No descendants),	Spouse takes all
IV Descendants only (No spouse)	Descendants take all
V Parents (No spouse or descendants)	Parents take all
VI Parents' descendants[3] (No spouse, descendants or parents)	Parents' descendants take all
VII Grandparents or their descendants[4] (No spouse, descendants, parents, siblings)	a) Paternal grandparents or their descendants share half b) Maternal Grandparents or their descendants share half
VIII None of the above survive.	State takes all[6]

[1] By at least 120 hours.

[2] Children, grandchildren, great-grandchildren, etc.

[3] Deceased's brothers, sisters, nephews, nieces, grandnephews, grandnieces, etc.

[4] Deceased's uncles, aunts, first cousins, first cousins once removed.

[5] In addition, the spouse takes all of the deceased's community property.

[6] When the deceased is not survived by any persons in categories I thru VII, his or her intestate probate estate escheats to the deceased's state of domicile.

Source: Uniform Probate Code

Several states have adopted formulas which differ from the Uniform Probate Code. In Minnesota, for example, if there are surviving children, the surviving spouse inherits the first $70,000 of the probate estate plus one-half of the remaining estate. In Iowa, the surviving spouse is entitled to inherit all of the real estate if the deceased left no children other than those of the spouse. In Wyoming, for example, the spouse takes half of the estate.

In general, the state-specified share for a surviving spouse recognizes his or her needs and is fairly consistent with what is provided in the wills of most married couples. It is important to note, however, that under state intestacy laws domestic partners, close friends, charitable organizations, and other unrelated individuals or groups receive nothing.

INHERITANCE BY ILLEGITIMATES

Most states have laws that deal specifically with the inheritance rights of persons born out of wedlock, and recent judicial decisions have caused these statutes—as well as the Uniform Probate Code—to be revised. The code now specifies that the marital status of parents, as far as children are concerned, is irrelevant for inheritance purposes. This means that a person born out of wedlock has the right to inherit as long as the relationship between child and parent can be established.

State laws very widely as to the kind of proof necessary to establish the parent-child relationship. For example, Florida law provides that an illegitimate child is a lineal descendant of his or her mother and is one of the natural kindred of the mother. The child is also a natural heir of his father if:

- the natural parents participated in a marriage ceremony before or after the out-of-wedlock birth, even though the attempted marriage is void;
- the paternity of the father is established by court order either before or after the father's death;
- the paternity of the father has been acknowledged in writing by the father.

INHERITANCE BY ADOPTED CHILDREN, FOSTER CHILDREN, AND STEPCHILDREN

State laws governing inheritance by adopted children vary widely in scope. For purposes of inheritance, the Uniform Probate Code regards an adopted person as the child of the adopting parent and the adopting person as the parent of the adopted child. But the adopted child is no longer considered a child of his natural parents unless, of course, the child is adopted by the spouse of the natural parent.

Under the code, foster children and stepchildren cannot inherit any part of an intestate estate. California, however, regards the relationship between a foster child or a stepchild and the foster parent or stepparent as the same as if it were an adoptive relationship, provided that two conditions are met. First, the relationship must have begun when the child was a minor and must have continued through the parent's lifetime. Second, there must be clear and convincing evidence that the foster parent or stepparent would have adopted the child had there not been a legal barrier to the adoption.

INHERITANCE BY ALIENS

Both the Uniform Probate Code and the laws of many states do not disqualify persons from inheriting under intestacy merely because they are aliens. Nevertheless, there may be a practical problem in distributing a share of the estate to an alien heir who resides in a country that does not maintain a diplomatic relationship with the United States, because Treasury Department regulations prohibit or restrict the transmittal of funds to the nationals of certain countries. Current lists of countries having reciprocal rights of inheritance, published by the U.S. Treasury and State Departments, should be consulted in these circumstances.

One approach used by estate administrators in Florida, when inheritance funds cannot be distributed or transferred to a Cuban national or a resident of Cuba, is to place the money in a "blocked account," which, if not claimed within a specified time, is treated as abandoned (like an unclaimed bank account) and escheats to the state.

INHERITANCE BY MURDERERS

In many states a person who unlawfully kills or participates in causing the death of the deceased cannot inherit from the deceased, either under intestacy law or as a will-designated beneficiary. The portion of the estate to which such a person would otherwise be entitled passes to those persons who would be entitled to it had the killer predeceased the deceased.

SURVIVAL OF THE BENEFICIARY

Although, as we noted in Chapter 10, one must survive the deceased in order to inherit from him, common law does not specify the length of time of survival. Any measurable length of time, such as one minute—or, theoretically, one second—is sufficient. Hence, when the survival of an heir affects the inheritances of other heirs, the timing of the death may become a hotly contested issue.

In an attempt to resolve the problem, many states have adopted the Uniform Simultaneous Death Act, which specifies that "when there is no sufficient evidence that persons have died otherwise than simultaneously, the property of each person shall be disposed of as if he had survived." The act does not, however, totally solve the problem because it implies that if there *is* adequate proof of the sequence of deaths, the surviving heir, no matter how brief the time of survival, will be entitled to his share of the deceased's estate.

Suppose, for example, that a couple in a second marriage, each with children from their first marriages, own their home jointly and die together in a plane crash. Since it cannot be established who survived (if only for a few seconds), a dispute is likely to arise among the children. If the wife's children can somehow prove that she survived her husband, the jointly owned home becomes part of her probate estate and goes to her children and not to his. Under the Simultaneous Death Act, however, *both* husband and wife survive each other, and hence one half of the home remains in each estate and passes, via state intestacy laws, to each spouse's children.

A provision of the Uniform Probate Code eliminates this problem in most situations. Borrowing from a frequently used estate-planning tactic, the code requires that in order to qualify as a beneficiary a person must survive the deceased by at least 120 hours. This provision substantially reduces litigation over who has survived the deceased.

PRE-DEATH GIFTS TO HEIRS

Assets distributed to an heir during the lifetime of the deceased can raise questions as to whether the assets were an outright gift or an advancement against the heir's ultimate inheritance and hence to be deducted from it. Because the transferring document—if, indeed, one exists—rarely specifies the donor's intent, litigation may result.

The Uniform Probate Code both clarifies and restricts the application of the advancement principle. It specifies that a gift will be considered an advancement only if the donor declares it as such "in a contemporaneous writing" or if the recipient acknowledged in writing that the gift constituted an advancement. This provision eliminates the problem of proving intent by requiring the intent to have been documented.

LOCATING THE HEIRS AT LAW

The administrator of the intestate estate is required to exercise diligence in identifying and locating the heirs at law, but this may not be important if it is clear that under state intestacy laws the shares specified for a surviving spouse or children will exhaust the probate assets. On the other hand, if the estate is substantial, identifying all the heirs at law is essential, and this may not be an easy task. Close relatives are generally easy to locate, but more distant ones—alienated siblings, or nieces and nephews—can be more difficult. After communicating with known family members, the administrator may find some of the following sources helpful in the search:

- birth certificates, marriage applications, and death certificates;
- military records, obtainable from the Department of Defense;
- government records, such as those maintained by the Bureau of the Census, the Social Security Administration, and the IRS;
- private institutional records: hospitals, churches, cemeteries;
- records maintained by private employers, unions, of trade associations;
- civic and fraternal organizations;
- family records, such as family bibles, family trees, or correspondence;
- court records of adoptions, dissolution of marriages, or probate administration.

Many of these organizations require special authorization for the release of confidential information. They may require copies of the administrator's letters of authority or the completion of a detailed application form, which they provide.

The administrator may also employ a private investigator or a genealogist to search for heirs, paying their fees with estate funds or from the inheritance to be received by the discovered heir. But this decision should be made with care, because a long-drawn-out search may prove expensive. The estate may be better served by a genealogist who specializes in searching for heirs than by a private investigator who specializes in other civil matters.

Genealogists generally charge for their services either on a per job, a per diem, or a contingent fee basis. Each method has its pros and cons and should be analyzed carefully before a commitment is made. If the heirs are likely to be located easily, the per diem basis is preferable. On the other hand, if the search is likely to be demanding, the contingent fee (usually amounting to one-fifth to one-half of the inheritance, depending on the size of the inheritance) is likely to be less expensive, since this fee may cover all of the investigator's costs of travel, investigation, and the preparation of documentary proofs. In any event, the administrator should bear in mind that all reasonable leads should be followed but it is not necessary to prove the identity of heirs at law to the exclusion of every possible doubt.

APPOINTMENT OF GUARDIAN AND CONSERVATOR

If the deceased left orphaned minor children, the court is required to appoint a guardian who will act *in loco parentis* until they reach the age of majority. This step is essential because minor children— in most states individuals under the age of 18—not only need to be provided with food, shelter, supervision, and guidance, but also are legally incapable of enrolling in school, consenting to medical or dental treatment, marrying, enlisting in the armed services, or engaging in a number of other activities without the consent of a parent or guardian.

In addition to the regular parental responsibilities, the guardian assumes responsibility for whatever inheritance was left to the children, but if this inheritance is substantial (more than $5,000 in some states) the court may also appoint a conservator—an individual or a bank or other financial institution—to manage these assets. There is no legal reason, however, why the appointed guardian cannot petition the court for appointment as the conservator as well because, unless the assets are quite complex, no great financial acumen is required. When the child reaches the age of majority, however, the assets automatically go to him, regardless of his maturity in using them.

Although in cases of intestacy the court is empowered to appoint as guardian anyone it chooses after a hearing that all interested persons attend, it usually appoints the guardian on the basis of bloodlines. That is, the person appointed is usually the child's or children's closest relative. But anyone appointed has the right to decline the appointment on grounds of age, financial stress, or for no reason at all. In such circumstances, the court must make another appointment. The person accepting the appointment will be issued letters of guardianship certifying that the guardian is entitled to act in all respects in place of the deceased parent or parents.

Because the court is expected to make the appointment "in the best interests of the child," any interested person—grandparents, aunts, or uncles, for example—can challenge the appointment of someone they regard as manifestly unsuitable. In addition, in all states a minor 14 years of age or older may challenge the appointment of a guardian, either before or after the appointment has been made, and may propose an alternative guardian. Priority will be given to this nominee if he or she seems suitable to the court.

CLOSING THE ESTATE

As we have noted, the administrator's responsibilities in settling an intestate estate are virtually the same as those of an executor with respect to a testate estate. Like the executor, he must handle creditors' claims, pay taxes and administration expenses, render an accounting to interested persons, distribute the remaining assets to entitled persons, and close the estate.

If, after the intestate estate is closed, a will of the deceased's is discovered, it is of no value to will-designated beneficiaries. The Uniform Probate Code provides no remedies for would-be beneficiaries under a will discovered after the administration of an intestate estate.

～ **12** ～
SETTLING A TRUST

Since you have been designated as the executor of the estate, it is quite likely that you have also been designated as the trustee or successor trustee of a revocable living trust that the deceased established before death. In this chapter we assume that you are a trustee. But even if someone else has been designated as the trustee, you may be called on for advice, although strictly speaking the settling of a trust is not your responsibility as executor. Hence, you need to understand what a trust is and how it can be settled on the death of the person who established it.

Basically, a trust is a legal entity (rather like a corporation) that is permitted to own, manage, and ultimately distribute any kind of real or personal property. The property it holds is transferred into trust ownership by the owner, known as the *settlor* or *grantor*. The trust assets, called the *trust estate*, are administered by one or more *trustees* for the current or future benefit of one or more *beneficiaries*.

The most widely used form of trust, the revocable living trust (see p. 44), has four very significant characteristics that have led to its increasing use as an estate planning tool.

First, all three roles—settlor, trustee, and beneficiary—can be filled by the same person or persons, but the settler can, at any time prior to his incompetency or death, place other persons in the roles of trustee and beneficiary. This means that during his lifetime, the settler who acts as his own trustee can move assets into or out of trust ownership, can use the trust assets or their yield for whatever purpose he chooses, and can change not only the designated beneficiaries but also the terms and conditions under which they receive their inheritances. In addition, the settler may, if he wishes, name another individual or entity (such as a bank or a trust company) to serve as trustee or successor trustee should he decide that someone else can manage the trust assets more skillfully.

Second, on the death of the settlor, trust assets are not considered part of the deceased's probate estate, and hence are not probatable. Under the control of the trustee and according to the terms of the trust document, they are held for or distributed to the designated beneficiaries free of probate court administration. This feature also provides both the deceased and the beneficiaries with a substantial measure of privacy, since the terms of the trust document need not be disclosed to anyone except the trustee and the beneficiaries, whereas probate administration of an estate is a public record open to the press and to anyone else, no matter what their interest.

Third, a trust can serve as the settlor's primary (and perhaps sole) beneficiary. That is, the settlor's will can direct that on his death all or a portion of his probate assets be "poured over" into the trust. This tactic does not avoid probate of the poured-over assets, but it assures the settlor far more post-death control over his assets than can be achieved through joint ownership or through a will that bequeaths assets to the beneficiaries immediately, directly, and unconditionally.

For example, if assets are bequeathed through a simple will to a son aged 19, the son would acquire total control of them immediately on completion of probate. Similarly, assets held in joint ownership with a spouse pass immediately to the surviving spouse, even if she remarries a day after her husband's death. A trust, by contrast, can direct that distribution of the assets be postponed until the son is graduated from college or reaches the age of 25 (or any other age), or that, upon remarriage, the spouse receive income only from the trust assets until her death, and that the assets themselves be distributed to the children.

Lastly, a trust can outlive the settlor by many decades and thereby extend the deceased's control of his assets for many years. In this way some or all of the settlor's assets, or income from them, can be passed on not only to his living beneficiaries but also to future generations under the conditions specified in the trust document.

FUNDING A TRUST

Establishing a revocable living trust sufficient to avoid probate of one's assets requires two steps. First, the settlor signs the trust document, which is usually prepared by lawyer skilled in estate planning so that it conforms with all legal requirements and meets the settlor's individual needs. Second, the settlor transfers into the trustee's name all or part of the assets which he owns in his name alone or, with the consent of his spouse, assets owned jointly with her. Those assets that are transferred to the trustee are not probatable, but any of the assets that the settlor does not transfer *are* probatable unless they avoid probate through joint ownership, by contract (such as Keogh accounts, IRAs, transfer-on-death accounts, or life insurance policies) or because their value is low enough to qualify for available small-estate transfer procedures (see Chapter 6).

But there are two variations to this typical pattern of which you need to be aware. First, the settlor may have had a trust document prepared and signed but then may have neglected, for one reason or another, to transfer any assets to its trustee. Such an unfunded or "dry" trust is inoperative and may be completely disregarded.

A second variation is the use of a will containing a "pour-over" clause. In this situation, the trust remains unfunded or partially funded until the death of the settlor, at which time the settlor's will designates the trustee of the trust as his primary beneficiary and directs that all his probate assets are to be "poured over" into the trust. In such a situation, all the poured-over assets are subject to probate, and, until they have been transferred to the trustee of the trust, you will deal with them in your role as executor. Once you have distributed those assets to the trustee, however, they become the exclusive responsibility of the trustee.

In some circumstances a trust funded by a "pour-over" will makes sense. In some states, for example, trust assets remain subject to creditors' claims, whereas in probate administration these claims may be disallowed if they are not filed within the specified claims period (see Chapter 8).

In most circumstances, however, the unfunded trust simply fails to achieve probate avoidance, for one or more of the following reasons:

- The settlor uses a do-it-yourself trust kit and overlooks the need to transfer his assets to the trustee of the trust;
- The settlor signs the trust document but he (or his lawyer) feels that, because he is young, he can postpone the funding

until death seems imminent. This, of course, overlooks the possibility of premature death;

- The settlor signs a trust document and funds it. Subsequently, however, he buys a new home or makes major changes in his investments but neglects to title or retitle them in the name of the trustee.

FINDING THE TRUST DOCUMENT

Obtaining a copy of the trust document is crucial to its settlement, since the document will (1) identify the trustee or successor trustee, (2) specify the trustee's powers and, possibly, the method of compensation, (3) list some or all of the trust assets or specify their whereabouts, (4) identify the trust's beneficiaries and, (5) specify what amounts they are to receive, when they are to be received, and any conditions that may be attached.

If you have been designated as the trustee or successor trustee, it is likely that the deceased informed you about its existence and the whereabouts of the trust document, or gave you a copy and obtained your signature on it signifying your consent to act as trustee. If, however, you do not have access to a copy, you may find a clue to its existence in the deceased's letter of instruction or in his will, either of which may contain instructions about pouring over assets into the trust. If these documents yield no results, you might consult the deceased's lawyer, accountant, or banker, check the contents of the deceased's safe deposit box, or review the deceased's other important personal papers. Some states provide a means of registering a trust with the probate court, in which case a call to the court in the country of the deceased's residence may disclose its existence and produce a copy.

ROLE OF THE TRUSTEE
AND SUCCESSOR TRUSTEE

Whether you served as trustee or cotrustee during the deceased's lifetime or became a successor trustee as a result of his lack of interest, disability, or death, your responsibilities are essentially the same—that is, to settle the trust in accordance with the instructions embodied in the trust document and in state laws governing trusts. In many ways, settling a trust as a trustee is similar to settling an estate as an executor. The steps include

- identifying and assembling the trust assets and ascertaining their value;
- investing the trust assets to achieve the maximum return consistent with safety of capital;
- obtaining a taxpayer identification number to use in filing any required tax returns for the trust;
- paying the trust's debts, expenses, and taxes; and
- distributing the remaining trust assets to the trust's beneficiaries according to the instructions contained in the trust document.

But the difference between this process and settlement through probate-court administration is extremely important. Because in most cases none of your activities in connection with the trust is subject to direct supervision by the probate court, the trustee is much freer to manage, hold, buy, sell, or otherwise deal with the trust assets than he would be under the generally conservative oversight by the probate court. The trustee's management of the trust assets is limited only by the wording of the trust document and state laws governing trusts. It is important to note, however, that the trust's beneficiaries can file a lawsuit against the trustee for mismanaging the trust assets, for self-dealing, for embezzlement, or for failing to carry out the directives contained in the trust document.

TRUSTEE'S FEES AND EXPENSES

As a trustee, you are entitled to a fee for your services in managing and settling the trust. A reasonable fee takes into consideration your qualifications and expertise, the nature of your duties and the time and effort they require, and the complexity and value of the trust's assets. If there is more than one trustee, the fee should be apportioned according to the duties and responsibilities of each of them. In some states the trustee's fees are set by statute requiring "reasonable" compensation or a percentage of the value of the trust assets.

If, in addition to serving as a trustee, you are also a trust beneficiary, it may be to your advantage to serve without fee, because the trustee's fee is taxable as income, whereas as a trust beneficiary your receipt of the trust assets is not subject to income tax.

IS A LAWYER NEEDED?

A major reason for establishing a trust is to reduce or eliminate probate administration and thus reduce or eliminate legal fees and expenses. If the trust estate is relatively small, the trust document clear and simple, and there are no complications, you should be able to settle the trust without having to retain a lawyer. In most cases, however, you should probably consult a lawyer experienced in estate and trust matters. And you should always consult a lawyer (and perhaps a certified public accountant) if it is necessary for the trust to file a federal income or estate tax return, or if the trust assets are subject to state inheritance or estate tax (see Chapter 9).

Reasonable legal, accounting, and other professional fees are payable from trust assets, and they are tax deductible against income and estate taxes.

ASSEMBLING THE TRUST ASSETS

Unless the trust document actually lists the assets held by the trust or indicates where a list of these assets may be found, identifying the trust assets involves essentially the same efforts that were described in Chapter 5. Bear in mind, however, that you are seeking only those assets that were transferred by the deceased to the trustee or successor trustee. The following listing can be used to guide your search for trust-held assets:

Real estate: a property deed or a land-contract assignment conveying the deceased's home, office, rental property, vacation home, or vacant land to "John Doe, Trustee of the John Doe Trust";

Personal property: a statement in the trust document itself, a list attached to the trust, or a separate assignment document specifying that the deceased's household goods, furnishings, and other contents are held in the name of "John Doe, Trustee of the John Doe Trust";

Bank accounts: checking or savings accounts, certificates of deposit, or other bank, credit union, or savings and loan

accounts held in the name of "John Doe, Trustee of the John
Doe Trust";

Securities: stock certificates, brokerage accounts, and mutual
funds held in the name of "John Doe, Trustee of the John
Doe Trust";

Vehicles: automobiles, motorcycles, mobile homes, and boats
with a certificate of title or a registration in the name of
"John Doe, Trustee of the John Doe Trust";

Business assets: equipment, supplies, accounts receivable, and
leases held in the name of "John Doe, Trustee of the John
Doe Trust."

COLLECTING PAYABLE ASSETS

As trustee, you are responsible not only for assembling the assets
that are clearly trust property but for collecting those assets that
are payable to the trustee on the death of the deceased. These
include:

Life insurance policies on the deceased's life that designate the
beneficiary as "Trustee or Successor Trustee of the John Doe
Trust" or words of similar effect;

IRA, SEP, Keogh, or 401K accounts or annuity contracts
owned by the deceased that designate the beneficiary as
"Trustee or Successor Trustee of the John Doe Trust";

The deceased's pension plan, profit-sharing plan, or other
work-related benefits which, by contract, are payable on
death to the "Trustee or Successor Trustee of the John Doe
Trust."

If, for example, the deceased left a life insurance policy that designates the beneficiary as "Trustee or Successor Trustee of the John
Doe Trust," you, as trustee, must file with the insurer a claim for the
death benefits. The claim form can be obtained from the local agent
or the claims department of the insurer, and it should be submitted
together with a copy of the trust document evidencing your authority to collect the money and a certified copy of the deceased's death
certificate.

If the deceased left probate assets to be poured over into the
trust through his will, these assets are subject to probate. In this situation, you, as trustee, must await the completion of probate

administration before collecting these assets and adding them to the trust estate for management and distribution according to the trust document.

The entire process of assembling and collecting the trust assets must be carried out just as carefully and conscientiously as the process of collecting and administering probate assets. Although the settlement of a trust is not generally supervised by any court, the trustee of a trust has virtually the same fiduciary responsibilities as does the executor of a probate estate.

VALUATION OF THE TRUST ASSETS

The trust assets must be appraised, for several reasons. First, if the assets in a revocable living trust plus any of the deceased's assets not held in the trust amount to more than $675,000[1] the trustee must file a Federal Estate Tax Return (IRS Form 706) and pay any estate tax (see Chapter 9). The will or the trust document may specify whether the taxes are to be paid by the trust estate or by the probate estate.

Second, the deceased's state of residence may impose an inheritance or estate tax on the value of assets transferred at death by use of a revocable living trust.

Third, a valuation is necessary to determine a new cost basis for the trust assets so as to take advantage of their stepped-up value and thus minimize any capital gains tax when the assets are ultimately sold. If, for example, the trust includes shares of the XYZ Corporation, which the settlor originally bought at $15 but which have risen to $35 at the time of death, the stepped-up basis becomes $35 rather than $15.

Fourth, if the trust document directs distribution of the assets to the beneficiaries on a percentage basis, a valuation is essential to determine the respective percentages.

The value of real estate can be established by reference to sale prices of comparable properties by use of valuations established by taxing authorities, or by a written estimate from a realtor or an appraiser. A realtor may provide this service without charge if he

---

[1] The estate tax exclusion amount, which is $675,000 for deaths during 2000 and 2001, is indexed for inflation up to 2006, when it reaches $1 million (see Table 9.2, p. 164).

anticipates getting the listing if and when the property is placed on the market. An appraiser, however, will charge a fee.

The current market prices of stocks and bonds are readily obtainable from the stock tables of any major newspaper published on or near the date of death. A clipping of the newspaper page, including the date, constitutes adequate evidence.

MANAGING AND INVESTING TRUST ASSETS

Although some trust documents specify immediate distribution of the trust assets to the designated beneficiaries, many trusts have a lifetime measurable in years—and sometimes in decades. Hence, the trustee, must be prepared to manage the trust assets over a considerable length of time, during which market conditions may change dramatically. Therefore, you may feel it necessary to shift and reinvest the trust assets from time to time.

In managing the trust assets, the trustee, like the executor of a probate estate, is subject to the "prudent man" rule. As it applies to trustees, this rule has been characterized as follows:

> All that can be required of a trustee . . . is that he shall conduct himself faithfully and exercise sound discretion. He is to observe how men of prudence, discretion, and intelligence manage their own affairs, not in regard to speculation, but in regard to the permanent disposition of their funds, considering the probable income, as well as the probable safety of the capital to be invested.
>
> Justice Putnam, writing in the 1830 Supreme Court decision of *Harvard College v. Amory*.

The trustee must act and invest in good faith, doing what prudent people would do in managing their own affairs. He must avoid speculation and undue risk of loss and provide a dependable income for the trust beneficiaries, while considering the safety of the capital for those who will benefit on termination of the trust.

INVESTING TRUST ASSETS

The trustee is responsible for investing the trust assets in ways that both preserve them and maximize their yield. If the trust document specifies the kinds of investments that the trustee may consider, the trustee is free to follow these specifications but must nevertheless do what he can to exercise prudence. Trust-authorized investments may include margin accounts, commodities, short sales, real estate, the operation of a closely held business, and other speculative investments. If the types of investment powers granted to the trustee are specified in the trust document, the trustee is not bound by any state-imposed restrictions on investments.

In some cases, however, the court may permit the trustee to deviate from the trust provisions if compliance appears to be impossible or if, because of circumstances not known to or anticipated by the settlor, strict compliance would defeat or substantially impair the accomplishment of the trust's basic purposes. An example of court-permitted deviation involved the estate of the newspaper magnate Joseph Pulitzer. Although Pulitzer prohibited his trustee from selling the shares of a publishing company, the trust beneficiaries were able to show the court that the publishing company was not operating profitably and that the trust assets invested in it would be wasted by bankruptcy or dissolution.

If, however, the trust document does not delineate the scope of the trustee's investment discretion, the trustee must work within the limits imposed by state law. On the one hand, the trustee is obligated to keep the trust estate productive by investing trust funds within a reasonable time of receiving them. For example, a trustee who failed to rent the deceased's condominium for four years was charged by the court with neglect of duty to obtain income for the trust and was ordered to compensate the trust estate for the consequent losses.

On the other hand, the trustee is not permitted to engage in speculative investments. In some states, the legislatures have established what is known as a *legal list*—that is, a listing of the types of investments that trustees may engage in. Although these lists vary from state to state, most of them restrict investments to federally insured instruments or accounts or to government-issued bonds. In addition, some states have enacted the Uniform Trustee's Powers Act, which specifies the powers granted to trustees.

Whatever the restrictions, however, the trustee should be aware of certain circumstances that can affect all investments. These are particularly significant if the trust is expected to remain in existence over a period of several years.

INFLATION AND INTEREST RATES

No matter how safe they may appear, fixed-dollar investments—in bonds and mortgages, for example—will decrease in value over the years as a result of inflation. Other types of investments—in stocks, for example—may increase in value over time, but this increase is illusory if it does not exceed the rate of inflation.

DIVERSIFICATION

The trustee who invests a large proportion of the trust assets in one security or one type of security is taking an undesirable risk. To protect the trust assets, it is preferable to divide the assets between some riskier investments (because of their higher yield) and some safer investments, even though these will generate a more modest return.

This balance can be achieved in two ways. First, an investment in a variety of mutual bond funds can produce significant diversification as well as professional management. Second, that proportion of the assets intended for the stock market can be invested in so-called "index funds," which provide diversification by investing broadly in the stocks that make up the Standard and Poor's 500, whose fluctuations are likely to reflect the behavior of the stock market as a whole.

NOTIFYING THE BENEFICIARIES

While you are assembling and investing the trust assets, it is necessary to notify all of the trust's beneficiaries about the trust assets they can expect to receive and about any conditions attached to their shares. The Uniform Probate Code (adopted in 16 states) requires a trustee to provide the beneficiaries with the following information:

The trustee's name and address, within 30 days of assuming the trusteeship;

Upon request from a beneficiary, a copy of the trust document and information about the trust's assets;

Upon request from a beneficiary, an annual accounting of the trust assets;

An account of trust assets when there is a change of trustees or when the trust terminates.

Any failure to communicate promptly and fully with the beneficiaries and to provide them with information about the trust, its assets, and their rights will, at best, foster distrust and incur disputes. At worst, it can lead to legal action that can result in your removal and liability for losses attributable to any breach of your responsibilities.

PAYMENT OF DEBTS, EXPENSES, AND TAXES

Unlike the executor of a probate estate, a trustee in some states has no obligation to notify the deceased settlor's creditors. In fact, because the settlor's assets now belong to the trustee, it is possible that the settlor's probate estate has no funds to pay his creditors and they may therefore go unpaid. If, however, the trust document or state law specifies that creditors be notified and that debts be paid from trust assets, creditors must be notified and paid.

If the deceased left probate assets in addition to assets held in the trust, you should coordinate your debt-settlement activities with the executor of the deceased's probate estate. If the deceased's will directs that all debts be paid from probate assets and the trust document is silent about the payment of debts, creditors should be paid only to the extent that the probate assets permit, and the trust assets should remain intact.

As the trustee, you are, of course, responsible for paying out of trust assets all obligations incurred by the trust—not only professional fees, commissions, and other expenses but also any mortgage payments, taxes, and insurance premiums on real estate or other assets held by the trust.

DISTRIBUTING TRUST ASSETS TO THE BENEFICIARIES

Once the trust assets have been assembled and evaluated, and all outstanding obligations (including taxes) have been satisfied, you are ready to distribute the trust assets to the beneficiaries exactly as specified in the trust document. The distribution process is essentially the same as that used in the distribution of probate assets (see Chapter 10).

Your delivery of trust assets to each beneficiary should be preceded by a signed receipt, which you should retain should it become necessary to prove to other beneficiaries, creditors, or other interested persons that delivery was in fact made.

Depending on the instructions contained in the trust document, it may be necessary for you to liquidate assets in order to effect distribution of the trust estate—especially if the trust document specifies monetary distribution but most of the trust assets consist of real property, securities, and other nonliquid assets. Your responsibility for obtaining maximum prices for trust assets is no different from that of the executor of a probate estate. That is, you can liquidate assets promptly without speculating as to whether the market will rise or fall.

Occasionally, however, it may be necessary for you to consider distributing certain assets in kind, even though the trust document directs distribution in money. For example, if one of the trust assets is a solely owned business or an interest in a partnership and there is simply no market for the sale of such an asset, the only realistic way in which the matter can be resolved is through distribution of the asset or the business interest to the particular beneficiaries. In such circumstances, full and candid discussion with the beneficiaries is essential to reaching a decision that is satisfactory to all of them.

FINAL ACCOUNTING

Although you have presumably provided the trust beneficiaries with interim accountings prior to distribution of the assets, it is advisable—indeed, required in some states—to provide each beneficiary with a final accounting, including income received and expenditures made up to the date of settlement. It is wise to obtain from each of the beneficiaries a receipt for this accounting so as to ensure that there is no subsequent question as to whether the accounting was, in fact, provided to them.

~ 13 ~

PROTECTING THE SURVIVORS

Although your formal duties as executor are discharged upon closing of the estate, you may wish to take some further steps to protect the beneficiaries, especially if the estate was a substantial one. Beneficiaries are usually confronted with three challenges: obtaining sound estate planning to assure efficient transfer of their estate to likely survivors, obtaining sound financial planning to protect and enhance their inheritance, and protecting themselves against financial exploitation.

Because actuarial figures indicate that most survivors of a marriage are women, and because some women are less sophisticated than men about finances, it may be especially important for you to maintain your interest in the situation and offer the surviving spouse the benefit of the experience you gained in settling the estate. But young beneficiaries—those who are legally adults but who may not yet have become fully mature—can also benefit from your help and advice.

REVISING THE WILL AND OTHER ESTATE PLANNING DOCUMENTS

Although the surviving spouse may have a valid will, the death is likely to require significant revision with respect to the bequests, the beneficiaries, and the nomination of an executor and, possibly, a guardian. Hence the survivor's will should be revised at the earliest possible moment, even though it may require further revision should she remarry. In the event of remarriage, for example, a revision of the will may be necessary to protect children of the first marriage. In addition, if the surviving spouse moves to another state—a common occurrence after a death—it is important that the will be revised to comply with the laws of the new state.

The will may also need revision to name a new guardian for minor children. Although the deceased's will may have designated a guardian, the surviving parent would automatically remain the legal guardian unless both parents died simultaneously—and hence the naming of the guardian may not have been particularly significant. Now, however, the death of the surviving parent may necessitate the appointment of a guardian, and this requires careful thought.

Three other important documents—the financial power of attorney, the living will or medical power of attorney, and the letter of instruction—should be revised if they already exist or created if they don't. The durable power of attorney, which presumably appointed the deceased spouse as agent, needs to be revised to designate as agent an adult son or daughter, some other relative who lives in the same vicinity, or a close friend.

The financial power of attorney, as well as the living will, or medical power of attorney, and the letter of instruction are discussed in Chapter 3.

AVOIDING PROBATE

Although joint ownership may have achieved probate avoidance of the deceased's assets, it leaves the surviving joint owner—usually the spouse—with sole ownership of assets that will, if nothing further is done, require probate on her death. Hence, she should be advised to convert her probatable assets into nonprobatable form as promptly as possible through one or more of the following estate-planning techniques.

JOINT OWNERSHIP

If the survivor has children or other relatives whom she intends to name as beneficiaries, one tactic for her consideration is to transfer solely owned assets into joint ownership—perhaps with an adult son or daughter. If not done carefully, however, this tactic may subject the donor to federal gift tax. Gift tax was not implicated in the creation of a husband-wife joint ownership because gifts between spouses are tax-exempt. But when joint ownership is created with a son, a daughter, or any other nonspouse, particularly with respect to real estate, half of the assets thus converted are regarded as a gift to the new joint owner and thus possibly subject to federal gift tax. However, if the amount transferred each year is less than $10,000 per donee, no gift tax is payable and, if the survivor is in reasonably good health, there is no reason why such $10,000 transfers cannot be made annually to each of her intended beneficiaries.

Of course, all the risks and disadvantages involved in joint ownership (see p. 37) apply here, and therefore it should be considered very carefully, especially when it involves nonspouses. But if the co-owners are trustworthy and the relationship is stable, this probate-avoidance tactic may prove simple and effective.

POD AND TOD ACCOUNTS

As we have noted in Chapter 3, pay-on-death and transfer-on-death accounts, two of the most efficient probate avoidance tactics, may be as useful for beneficiaries as they were for the deceased. They provide the beneficiary with full control of the assets during her lifetime and allow her to change beneficiaries at any time.

THE REVOCABLE LIVING TRUST

Although consumer protection agencies regularly receive complaints from individuals who have been victimized by salespersons offering to set up revocable living trusts, such an arrangement may be desirable if (1) the value of the assets is considerable, (2) the assets include real property located in another state, or (3) the survivor's marital situation is uncertain. If, for example, the survivor remarries and places assets in joint ownership with the new spouse, the children from the first marriage may be entirely disinherited. A trust, on the other hand, while giving the settlor complete discretion over the trust assets during his or her lifetime, can protect the children of a first marriage by designating them as exclusive or partial beneficiaries. It can also protect the settlor against loss of her assets in a second marriage that proves to have been ill advised. The revocable living trust is discussed in detail in Chapter 3.

LIFE INSURANCE POLICIES

If the surviving spouse had designated the deceased as a beneficiary on a life insurance policy, it is important to revise the beneficiary designation so that the contingent beneficiaries originally named in the policy are now designated as primary beneficiaries and other contingent beneficiaries can be added. If the designated beneficiaries are self-sufficient and the estate includes other assets, the survivor may consider cashing in or terminating life insurance policies, but maintaining them can be useful in creating funds to pay death taxes (see Chapter 9).

CHARITABLE ANNUITIES, REVERSE MORTGAGES

If the survivor has no beneficiaries in mind, and if immediate income is insufficient, a charitable annuity or a reverse mortgage may be advisable. A number of charitable and nonprofit organizations offer annuities payable for life to anyone who donates a substantial amount to them. And reverse mortgages, in which a bank or mortgage company assumes ownership of the home and pays the occupant monthly interest, may also be used to supplement an inadequate income.

INVESTING THE INHERITANCE

If the deceased nominated a trustee to manage the survivors' inheritance, or if the survivors are financially sophisticated, there is no need for you to involve yourself in providing financial advice. Unfortunately, these conditions do not prevail in many cases, and hence you may need to help the survivors invest their inheritance in ways that combine safety of capital with maximal yield and that take account of changes in interest rates.

The survivors may need help and advice on a number of issues: whether to keep or sell real estate, whether to hold or liquidate bequeathed securities, and how to divide household goods. If a dispute arises among the beneficiaries, the following solutions are possible:

1. The beneficiaries may amicably agree to exchange among themselves assignments of personal property or deeds of real property so that each receives what he really wants.
2. The beneficiaries, unable to agree on an exchange, may agree to sell everything, pay the expenses of the sale, and share the net proceeds.
3. If neither of these solutions is acceptable, it is possible to file a lawsuit seeking a court order to split up (or "partition") real

property or, alternatively, to order a forced sale, the net proceeds to be divided among the beneficiaries. This, however, is a
very expensive solution and should be a last resort.

SELLING INHERITED PROPERTY

Generally speaking, if you sell property that has appreciated in
value, the profit you earn is taxable as a capital gain. This capital
gain is the difference between your "tax basis" (what you paid for
the property plus improvements and commissions) and your net
receipts when you sell it. If you inherited the property, however,
through probate, via a living trust, or as the designated beneficiary
on a transfer-on-death securities account, your tax basis is the value
of the property on the date of the deceased's death, regardless of
what he paid for it or added to it.

If, for example, a person buys a home or a commercial building
in 1993 for $100,000 and adds improvements of $50,000, his tax
basis is $150,000. If he subsequently sells the building in 2001 for
$300,000, he has a capital gain of $150,000 on which he pays
income tax. If, however, he dies in 2000 and wills the building to a
survivor, the tax basis becomes the value of the property at the time
of death. If the survivor sells the building for $300,000, the sale
price is equal to the stepped-up tax basis and there is no capital gain
on which to pay income tax.

This is why it is extremely important for survivors to determine
the value of inherited assets as of the date of death and to keep
records of these values.

Assets passing to survivors by way of joint ownership, however,
do not enjoy a 100 percent stepped-up tax basis. For example, when
spouses own an asset jointly, the law regards each as owning half of
it. If the property described in our example above had been owned
jointly by the spouses, the survivor receives a stepped-up tax basis
only on the half that belonged to the deceased—that is, $75,000
stepped up to $150,000. The surviving spouse's tax basis of
$75,000 plus the stepped-up basis of the deceased's half
($150,000) brings the new tax basis to $225,000. If the property is
then sold for $300,000, there is a taxable gain of $75,000.

If the inherited property is a primary residence, there are additional tax aspects that should be considered. If the home is sold and
a new one is brought or built within the specified time period (cur-

rently two years), the entire profit from the sale is tax deferred if the new residence costs more than the sale price of the old one. This deferment applies to everyone, regardless of age. If, however, the survivor is over the age of 55, up to $250,000 of profit on the sale of a primary residence is exempt from tax, whether or not he or she buys a new home. This exemption can be used only once in a lifetime.

INVESTING IN SECURITIES

A most important issue involves the investment of cash in securities, and it is here that many beneficiaries commit serious errors.

In general, the safer an investment—that is, the lower the likelihood that part or all of it will be lost—the lower its yield. This is why savings accounts (which are insured against loss by the federal government) pay a lower rate of interest than money market funds (which are not insured), and why shares in such blue-chip companies as AHP or 3M pay lower dividends than shares in some smaller and less-established companies. It explains also why blue-chip shares are less likely to rise sharply than those of some new, aggressive, innovative companies. In short, just as one pays insurance premiums to minimize the loss of a home or a car, the lower yields on established companies represent a "premium" that protects the investment against shrinkage or obliteration.

The first decision the survivor must make, therefore, is what degree of risk he or she can afford. Money invested in shares of a fledgling corporation may be lost or sharply diminished, but it can also make the shareholder very rich.

The degree of tolerable risk depends, to some extent, on the age of the survivor. An elderly widow may prefer a conservative approach, choosing investments that offer relatively low earnings and little prospect of dramatic growth but that can be liquidated readily should the need arise. A young child's inheritance, on the other hand, since it is not needed immediately, might be invested in a combination of securities, some long-term and some short, some safe and some relatively risky. Although past performance is no guarantee of future performance, the stock market over a span of decades has proved to be highly rewarding.

THE QUESTION OF YIELD

Thus far we have been discussing yield in very general terms. Unfortunately, there is no way of designating a specific return—say 7 percent—as "good." The only way to assess a rate of return is to subtract from it the rate of inflation. Thus, if a savings account pays 3 percent and the rate of inflation is 3 percent, the deposit is not only earning no interest but the depositor is actually losing money, because income tax will have to be paid on this 3 percent return.

Of course, your yield on common stocks does not indicate your total return, because it includes only the dividends you receive. Your *total* return includes not only the dividends (which may fluctuate) but also the difference between the price when you bought or received it and the price at which you can sell it (which may also fluctuate).

GETTING ADVICE

No book can label any type of investment (money market funds, for example, or common stocks) or the stock of a specific company as a "best buy" for all investors. Hence, once the survivors have made some broad decisions on the basis of the general advice offered above, they may want to find an expert to help them invest their inheritance where it can best realize their goals in terms of safety, yield, and liquidity.

The Professionals
Unfortunately, although many people—stockbrokers, financial counselors, accountants, insurance salesmen, and others—label themselves as experts, their performance over the years does not justify this label. And this negative evaluation applies not only to many of the "experts" available to the small investor through local banks and brokerage firms, but also to many of those money managers who handle billion-dollar portfolios for pension funds and other mammoth-scale investors. Although many of them can legitimately boast of above-average performance over the course of a year or two, few, if any, have shown consistently superior results over a period that may equal the life expectancy of an inheritance.

On the other hand, the individual investor, whether he studies the market very carefully or operates purely by hunch, may not fare any better. It is not uncommon to hear, at cocktail parties, the success stories of individuals who have "made a killing" on the stock market. But people who have "taken a bath" on Wall Street may be just as numerous, even though they are unlikely to use their experience as material for small talk.

Doing It Yourself

A major mistake sometimes made by beneficiaries is to invest most or all of their inheritance in a single instrument, whether it be the bonds or shares of a favorite company or a recommended mutual fund. A better plan is for beneficiaries to put the money immediately into a safe and readily liquidable investment—a money market fund or a short-term U.S. Treasury obligation—and parcel it out gradually as they learn more about investing. If they set to work seriously, they will soon become familiar with the various investment alternatives and the ways of protecting their inheritances against serious losses.

They will not, of course, acquire this understanding by reading the perennial crop of books on how to make a fortune in the stock market or in gold trading. (Anyone familiar with the effort involved in writing and marketing a how-to-get-rich book will realize that if the author's system really worked, he would earn far more by practicing than by preaching it.) But there are a number of low-key, sensible books that explain investments objectively instead of touting a particular system or formula, and careful study of a number of them can make investing sensible and relatively safe. Learning about investing does take time, but it does not require inordinate intelligence.

Of course, stocks and bonds can be traded only through a broker, but a growing number of do-it-yourself investors use discount brokers—"no frills" firms that charge cut-rate commissions because they maintain no costly research departments and offer their customers no advice. Their account executives, being salaried order-takers, have no incentives to churn your account or to urge you to trade actively to maximize their commissions, but in most other respects they provide the same services as full-service brokers. Using such a firm can save you more than half the usual broker's commission every time you buy or sell a stock, and over the years this can amount to a significant sum of money that otherwise would be paying for services that are of no value to the do-it-yourself investor.

DIVERSIFYING

As we have noted, "putting all your eggs in one basket" is inadvisable when the "basket" is the shares of a single corporation or some other kind of investment, such as a U.S. Treasury bond. It is equally inadvisable when the basket is a single *type* of security—bonds, for example, or stocks, or money market accounts. The reason is that a shift in interest rates or market conditions can easily make a desirable investment undesirable.

Although experts differ on the percentage of an individual's assets that should be put into stocks, bonds, and cash, virtually all of them agree that a portfolio should include all three. Thus, when interest rates rise, the value of bonds falls, but the yield on money market accounts rises. And when the stock market drops, the value of bonds tends to rise. Hence, the safest approach is to hedge one's investment by diversifying it not only among stocks, bonds, and cash, but within these categories as well.

PROTECTION AGAINST EXPLOITATION

Whether they are young or old, survivors who receive substantial inheritances may be highly vulnerable to exploitation, especially if the deceased failed to establish a trust to protect the assets. According to complaints received by consumer protection agencies, widows are especially likely to be victimized. This is readily understandable, since many of them are not highly employable, are naive about investments, and, hence, are heavily reliant on their inheritances to maintain their standard of living.

The exploiter of widows, according to the stereotype, is a smooth talking confidence man or a fortune-hunting widower. Although such exploiters are not uncommon and frequently take advantage of the survivor's loneliness, another group—"investment advisors" and "financial planners" of various stripes—are probably much more dangerous, and more efficient. Because most states do not regulate this industry, almost anyone, regardless of qualifications, can assume the title of investment advisor or financial planner and proceed to victimize clients.

Because many of these advisors earn income not only from the fees they charge their clients but also from commissions paid for the various investment products they sell the client, the likelihood of a conflict of interest is high. This is, the investment advisor is likely to recommend securities that provide him or her with a commission but are not necessarily the most appropriate for the client.

Similarly, many stockbrokers who take on the accounts of widows have been accused of "churning" these accounts—that is, frequently moving in and out of securities at a substantial gain in commissions but at no advantage whatever to the client.

The problem is that many survivors fall into one of two categories. Some of them, insisting on the highest degree of safety attainable, concentrate all their assets in federally insured instruments and find themselves accepting a relatively low yield that is often diminished by inflation. On the other hand, some survivors, eager to maximize their income, are susceptible to high-risk investments that quickly drop in value.

The advice you offer will depend, of course, on the amount of the assets involved as well as on the survivor's sophistication and ability to accept risk. But, as we have noted, diversification is a crucial safeguard. In addition, unfaltering faith in the advice of a full-service stockbroker is probably unwarranted. Above all, unsolicited telephone sales pitches for investments should invariably be rejected, especially if they involve unlisted securities or "get-rich-quick" promises.

If the survivor's inheritance includes an existing stock portfolio, the question arises as to whether to retain or liquidate it. If the shares have appreciated substantially since their original purchase, they can be liquidated without the payment of capital gains tax, since their stepped-up tax basis is determined as of the deceased's date of death. The survivors may, of course, be tempted to retain what have historically proven to be "good" stocks, but it is important to note that no "good" stock is good indefinitely. Many investors have lost money on such blue chips as IBM and AT&T.

If the principal survivor is elderly and living alone, he or she is especially prone to respond to telephone solicitations involving all sorts of scams—notably fraudulent prize contests and other deceptive offers. Consumer protection organizations report that lonely elderly people have been fleeced of many thousands of dollars by these schemes. Although it may be difficult to achieve, an attempt should be made to cancel a chronically gullible elderly person's credit cards and to stipulate that the checking account require two signatures, the second being that of an adult child or other relative.

Because the death of a spouse is frequently followed by a household move—to smaller quarters or to another part of the country—sale of the existing home should be planned carefully and not done on the spur of the moment, since the impact of the death can lead to unwise decisions. For the same reasons, any move to another part of the country should be made tentatively, preferably by short-term rental, until the new location proves completely satisfactory.

INDEX